IMAGES
of America

PLANO'S HISTORIC CEMETERIES

IMAGES
of America

PLANO'S HISTORIC CEMETERIES

The Plano Conservancy
for Historic Preservation, Inc.

ARCADIA
PUBLISHING

Published by Arcadia Publishing
Charleston, South Carolina

Printed in the United States of America

Library of Congress Control Number: 2014935400

For all general information, please contact Arcadia Publishing:
Telephone 843-853-2070
Fax 843-853-0044
E-mail sales@arcadiapublishing.com
For customer service and orders:
Toll-Free 1-888-313-2665

Visit us on the Internet at www.arcadiapublishing.com

*This book is dedicated to Maggie Sprague and Russell Kissick,
founders of the Plano Conservancy for Historic Preservation, Inc.*

CONTENTS

Acknowledgments   6

Introduction   7

1.   Baccus Cemetery   9

2.   Bethany Cemetery   19

3.   Bowman Cemetery   31

4.   Routh Cemetery   45

5.   Plano Mutual Cemetery   57

6.   Rowlett Creek Cemetery   71

7.   Young Cemetery and Scatter Garden   83

8.   Collinsworth Cemetery   99

9.   Additional Historic Plano Cemeteries   111

ACKNOWLEDGMENTS

We wish to thank Jeff Campbell, Kirby Stokes, and Candace Fountoulakis for their dedication to researching, writing, supplying photographs, and designing the layout for this book.

We wish to acknowledge the generosity of the City of Plano and Cheryl Smith and Tom Turner of the Plano Public Library System for use of images from the Francis Bates Wells Collection as well as access to their other collections. We are also grateful for the assistance from the following people: Stacey Davis of the Richardson Public Library, Katherine Powers of the Frankford Cemetery Association, Susan Swain from the Mary Couts Burnett Library Special Collections at Texas Christian University, and Emily Miller of the Frankford Cemetery for her contributions.

We also wish to thank the Plano Conservancy for Historic Preservation, Inc. Board of Directors for its enthusiasm and support for this project: Russell C Kissick (codirector), Jeff Campbell (codirector), Sid Wall (president), Harry Kepner (vice president), Alexander "Pete" Schoemann (treasurer), Candace Fountoulakis (secretary), Amy Sandling Crawford, Duane Peter, Clint Haggard, Lauren Partovi, and Barbara Zepeda. We also wish to thank all of our volunteers who provided support and assistance during this project.

A special thanks goes to Robert Haynes, curator of Plano's Interurban Railway Museum, for his advice and guidance through the process of writing this book.

Gratitude also goes to Norwood Brenneke, Jeran Akers, the Plano City Council, the Plano Heritage Commission, and to all those whose names should be included in this list but are not. Please forgive us for this oversight. You know who you are, and we thank you, too.

Unless otherwise noted, images in this book appear courtesy of the Plano Conservancy for Historic Preservation, Inc. and the Genealogy Center at Haggard Library.

INTRODUCTION

When you stand beneath the shade of tall trees, a breeze coming over the hill to cool the body and soothe the soul, it is hard to envision the strength of will it must have required to settle in this place. Only nearby creeks, rich soil, and plentiful grass could convince the pioneer that North Central Texas, what we now know as Plano, might be the place to stop searching and put down roots. It certainly looks peaceful enough today, but when settlers arrived from Illinois, Kentucky, and Tennessee, there were ever-present threats to survival. Although attacks from native tribes were few and far between, they did occur, and rarely did the victims survive. Pioneers by their very nature were rugged individualists, but survival still required contact and cooperation with others. This very contact might be the beginning of the end if your neighbors turned out to be carrying a conventional weapon or a contagious disease. Childbirth was a very real death threat, and the loss of a mother inevitably reduced the likelihood of remaining children surviving for long. Injury, illness, starvation, and weather all conspired to kill off settlers before they could bring in their first crop. As so often happened, the spouse left behind remarried in a hurry and only had a small handful of prospects to choose from. The faith of these hardy folks sustained them through the devastation of death that they faced frequently. Landowners set aside an acre for a family cemetery and allowed their neighbors to make use of the same land when the need arose. The stories of those who succumbed quickly and those who lived long lives are told over and over again on the grave markers of these cemeteries. From small family plots to church graveyards and municipal burial grounds, Plano has a wealth of history buried beneath its fast-disappearing land. The pages of this book are designed to bring these old cemeteries "to life" in an effort to preserve their history, highlight their beauty, and introduce new generations to lives lived long ago.

FAMILY PLOTS
The year 1847 dates the graves of the two earliest marked burials in Plano. Both were pioneer family members who never saw their first birthday, and their mothers followed them in short order. The bereaved buried them in the dark soil of the prairie and the land around them became the place where relatives, friends, and neighbors were laid to rest. As the rural land changed hands and uses, barbed wire fences or other means of protecting the burial grounds were erected to keep out cattle and wild animals and to indicate the boundary of the cemeteries. Flowers, shrubs, and trees were planted to enhance the setting, and rudimentary maintenance was performed to make these sites inviting for people to visit and remember the dead. Many of the hardy species planted long ago still survive in the secluded corners of these cemeteries and bloom in season to this day.

CHURCHES AND SCHOOLS
Settlers formed churches and built schools and these were often side by side or in proximity to one another. The graveyards of long since departed congregations exist without the structures or religious

affiliations that founded them. The names of roads, parks, schools, and institutions well known to residents of present-day Plano can be found among those buried in its cemeteries. Unlike the flat standard grave markers in modern cemeteries, upright monuments in marble, sandstone, zinc, wood, and granite feature a variety of decorative types—from hand-carved markers, illustrating the limited schooling of the artisan, to machined renderings with elaborate inscriptions. A walk through an old cemetery should inspire the visitor and bring some to tears.

MEMORIAL PARKS
With the growth of towns and the need for larger cemeteries, memorial parks became popular places for not only remembering the dearly departed, but also as places to relax and enjoy nature in open space away from the noise, crowds, and activity of city life. Plano's history as a small town incorporated in 1873 did not lend itself to large cemeteries that are common among the original colonies and larger eastern cities, but more spacious burial grounds did replace family plots in town. These "municipal" cemeteries still resorted to separate sections or quarters that represented affiliations among those buried in them. Masonic temples set aside plots for their members and religious affiliation directed some burial locations. Race played a role as well, and the small but influential black population of Plano had its own burial grounds before modern assimilation dispersed concentration from segregated neighborhoods into the general populace.

We hope this trip through the pioneer cemeteries of Plano will ignite an interest in our history, as reflected in the tombstones that still stand in silent tribute to the settlers who braved the unknown and lived and died here long ago.

One

BACCUS CEMETERY

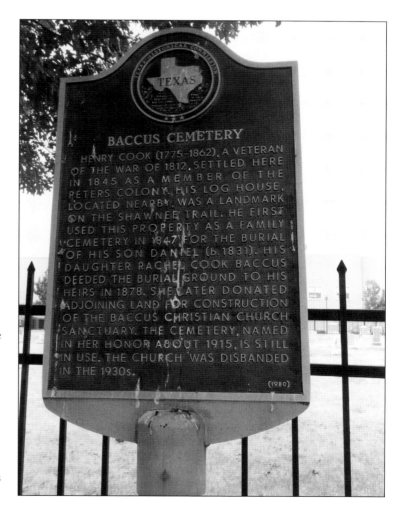

Receiving its historical marker from the state in 1980, Baccus Cemetery is located on the old remnants of the Shawnee Trail. The cemetery has survived many changes in its life, starting in 1847 and remaining in use today. Originally used as a small family plot, then expanded to a church cemetery, this resting place has always been looked after.

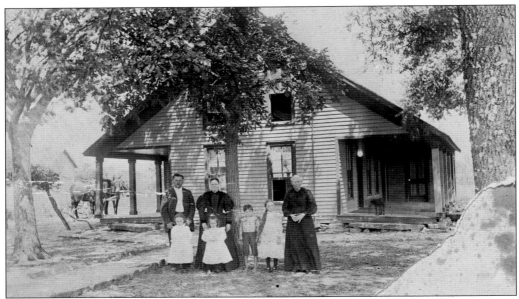

The Cook home was known as "the Lonesome House" and was somewhat of a legend in its time, serving as a lighthouse at night and a trail marker by day. The unique location was visible from all directions. Henry Cook was one of the founders of the Liberty Baptist Church, which was built west of the Cook home. Many travelers were beckoned by the lights and hospitality of the Cooks and the Liberty Baptist Church and would decide to stay the night before continuing on their journeys. The Cook family first maintained the cemetery property, followed by the local women. Those women eventually organized into a group that became an association. Currently, the cemetery is being maintained by the Baccus Cemetery Association, as well as being protected and revered by EDS, which is responsible for development of the area.

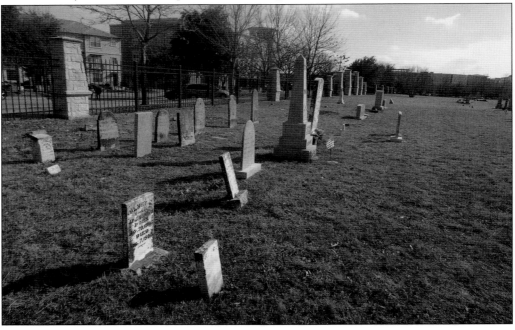

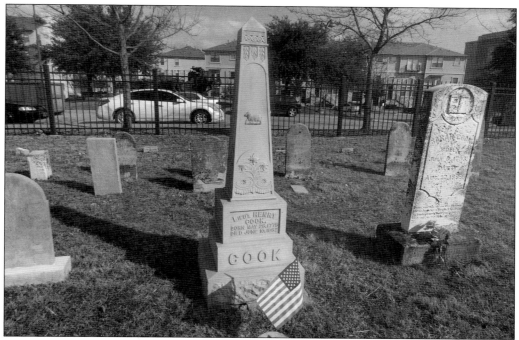

Henry Cook was born on May 28, 1775, in Virginia (now West Virginia), where he lived in a French settlement near a Native American village. He served as a lieutenant in the War of 1812 and was a French and Indian interpreter. On September 1, 1846, Cook left Virginia for Texas in a caravan of seven wagons. In the spring of 1847, the pioneers settled into what is now known as Plano, Texas. Cook remarried and is the known paternal point for two sets of six children; all settled in the Denton area and were within riding distance from Cook's home. Cook was a large and powerful personality and led a wagon train from Illinois to Texas at the age of 75. He passed away in 1862 and is buried with a prominent monument in the Baccus Cemetery.

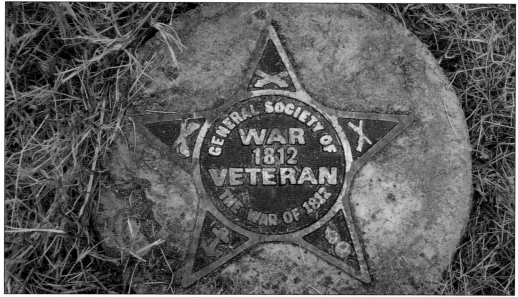

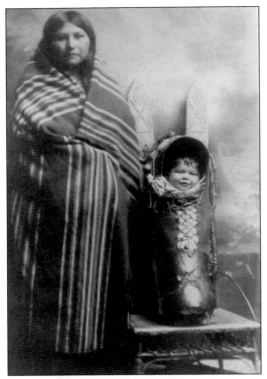

Henry Heustis was Henry Cook's son-in-law and a Confederate soldier. He was captured by Indians and held to be burned at the stake. A local Indian woman who had lost a son herself freed him and told him how to escape. He was to swim the river for the night and the next day, in order to give enough time for the warriors to give up their search. Then, after waiting overnight, he was to enter into the woods and run. He stated upon his return that he was so hungry, he thought to eat his hat, but luckily, he captured a wild fowl that he ate raw due to his starvation. Pictured here are an Indian woman and her child from a local tribe. (Left, courtesy of Clay County Jail Museum; below, courtesy of Kirby Stokes.)

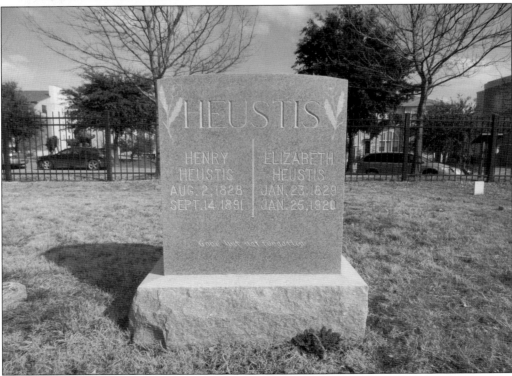

Rachel Cook Baccus is the descendant of Henry Cook who deeded the land to be used as a church and cemetery for future family members' final resting places. In 1915, the cemetery association responsible for the upkeep of the cemetery renamed it Baccus Cemetery (from Cook Cemetery) in honor of her generous gift. At its height of use, there were 285 marked graves here. The first was that of Daniel Cook, one of Henry Cook's sons; he was buried January 13, 1847. The second burial was another tragic loss of a child, this time being 16-month-old George W. Martin, who was buried August 17, 1850.

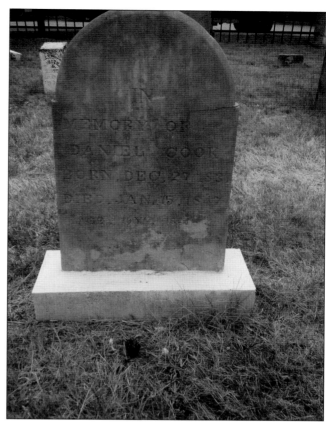

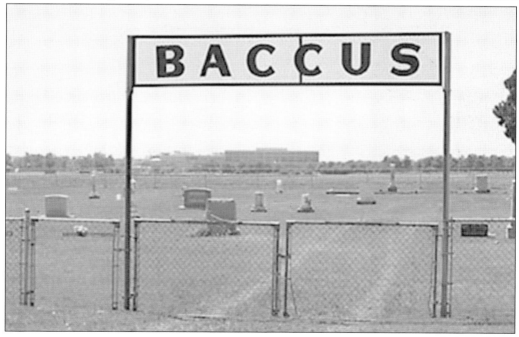

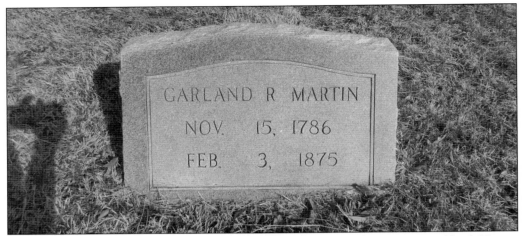

Garland Rhodes Martin came to Texas at 64 years old and is listed in a census as blind. He was married to Betsy Ann Richardson, and they traveled with their son John Berryman Martin. John was a carpenter and assisted in the construction of the Issac Young house as well as schoolhouses in the area. He was a soldier in the Mexican War and returned home to marry Martha Cook. Once settled back into the Plano area, he was elected as the commissioner of Collin County, followed by his election as justice of the peace. John was also a partisan Texas Ranger until the close of the Civil War.

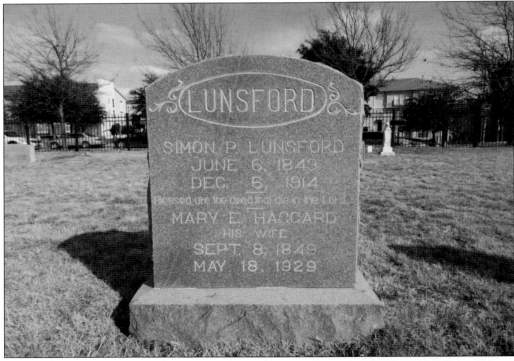

Simon Peter Lunsford traveled into Texas with his sister and their widowed mother. The surviving diary of Mary Susana Lunsford, Simon's sister, tells of their migration into Texas from Kentucky. The Lunsford family walked most of the trek, covering 9 to 25 miles a day. It rained a lot, and the mud and rising rivers constantly impeded their travels.

Isabelle Florence Thompson left Kentucky with her husband, Hugh Nelson, and their nine children. Originally, they were traveling by steamboat down the Mississippi River, and then Hugh hired an oxteam and wagon to continue onward. However, during this time, there was a raging cholera epidemic. One of the men traveling with the group heard there was a doctor within 20 miles and sent the eldest son to fetch him on horseback. When the boy and the doctor arrived back, all four infected children had already passed. The doctor attempted to work on the last child to pass and successfully brought back to life John Garland Thompson, who then lived into his 90s. Pictured here is a river much like the ones the Lunsford family would have encountered. The exact location of this photograph is unknown. (Below, courtesy of Marfa Public Library.)

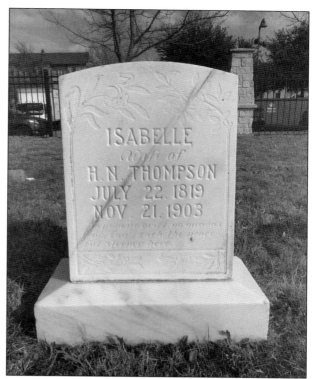

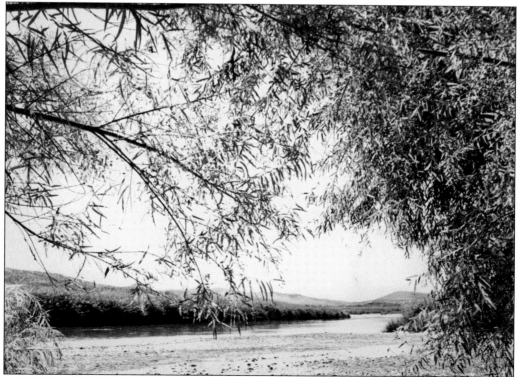

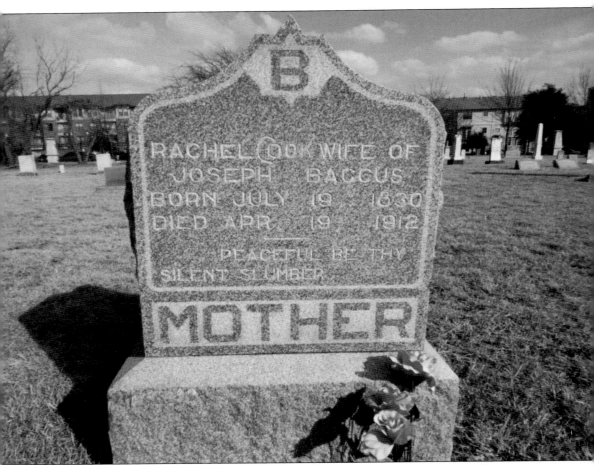

The Baccus family first appeared on the prairies of Plano in 1844. It was Godfrey Baccus and his wife, as well as Peter Baccus and John Baccus. They came with a team of eight caravans and settled on Rowlett Creek. The men would marry and have many children who would spread the name and prosperity of the Baccus family. Rachel Cook Baccus married Joseph Baccus, and this is where the name change from Cook Cemetery to Baccus Cemetery can be traced. The Baccus Christian Church was organized on July 1, 1908, and on May 8 1909, Rachel Baccus sold a tract of land for the sum of one dollar to be used for future church land. It is believed that the church was dissolved in the 1930s, but the building remained for many more years.

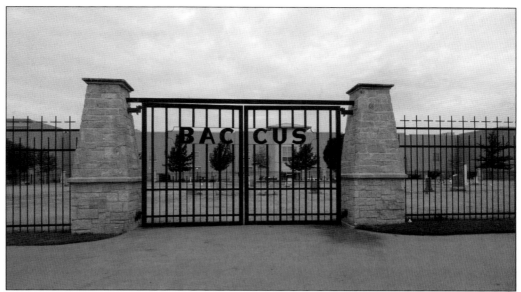

When Ross Perot purchased the 2,600 acres surrounding the cemetery, the EDS group did all its surveying from the cemetery land. When development began, large construction equipment was parked in the front of the cemetery. Anne Pearson called EDS and eventually got in contact with Robbie Robinson, the engineer in charge of development. He apologized for any unintended disrespect and had the equipment moved by the next day. Under Robinson's direction, a lot of honor was paid to the cemetery. Surrounding streets were designated names found on the tombstones. The Pearsons and the Robinsons became good friends, and Robbie was allowed to be one of the only nonfamily members to make Baccus Cemetery his final resting place.

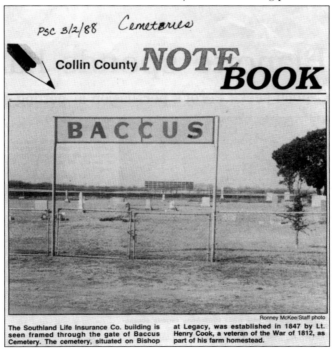

PSC 3/2/88   Cemeteries

Collin County NOTEBOOK

BACCUS

Ronney McKee/Staff photo

The Southland Life Insurance Co. building is seen framed through the gate of Baccus Cemetery. The cemetery, situated on Bishop at Legacy, was established in 1847 by Lt. Henry Cook, a veteran of the War of 1812, as part of his farm homestead.

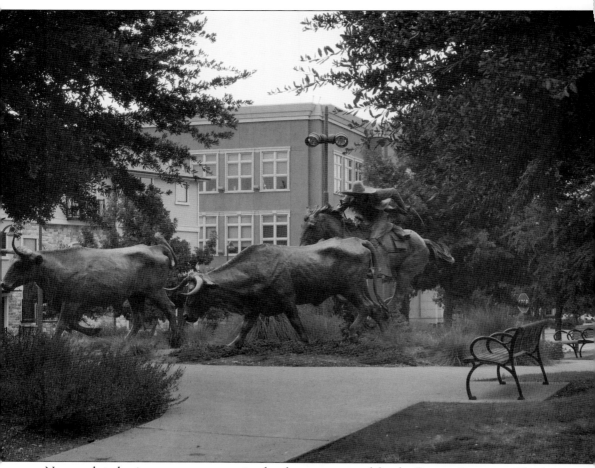

New work to begin a current renovation has been contracted for the Baccus Cemetery. Charles Bishop Pearson and his wife, Anne Kennedy Pearson, maintained the cemetery until the Legacy Association and EDS took over full-time. Charles and Anne's daughter Libby Pearson tragically passed away and is buried at Baccus Cemetery. The streets intersecting by the cemetery are named Libby Road and Pearson Drive in her honor. Six generations of Henry Cook's descendants are buried there and future generations will continue to use the land for this purpose. The longhorn bulls pictured here are sculptures created by Robert Summers; they are made of bronze, and there are a total of 22 statues in his depiction of a cattle drive.

Two

BETHANY CEMETERY

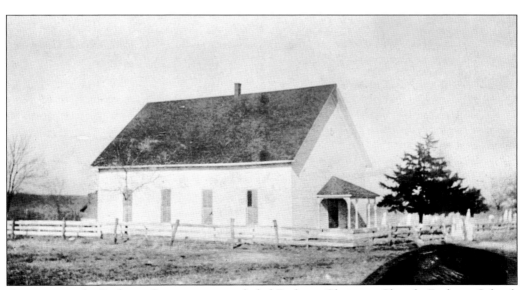

At one time, the Bethany Cemetery site included Bethany Christian Church, Bethany School, and the Bethany Home Demonstration Club. The cemetery is the final resting place for members of the Carpenter and Clark families. Burials began in 1877, and many gravesites are elaborately decorated with curbing.

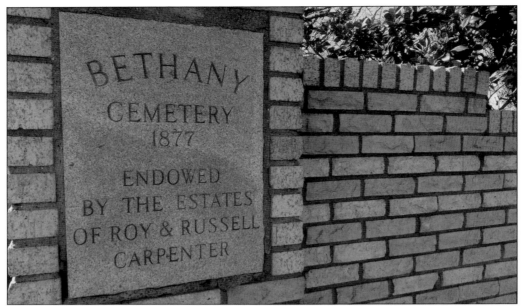

A granite panel pays tribute to Roy and Russell Carpenter. The Carpenters donated the land for the cemetery in 1877. Family patriarch R.W. Carpenter started the cemetery due to the infant death of Dick Clark's son. Clark's son was the first burial, and R.W. Carpenter's young daughter Catherine was the second burial. Another granite panel at the gates gives visitors a brief introduction to the history of the site, located six miles northwest of downtown Plano.

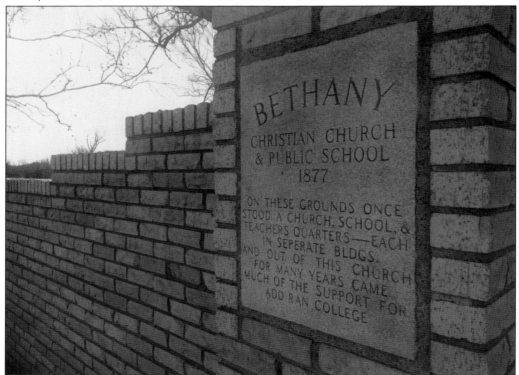

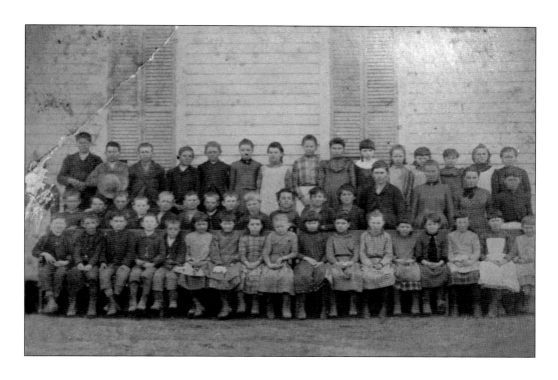

Both the Bethany School and the Bethany Christian Church were started in 1876. The church and school were both founded by R.W. Carpenter. The Bethany site was busy with many other community activities. The Bethany Canning Club was started in 1920. Later, in 1925, the Bethany Home Demonstration Club was founded.

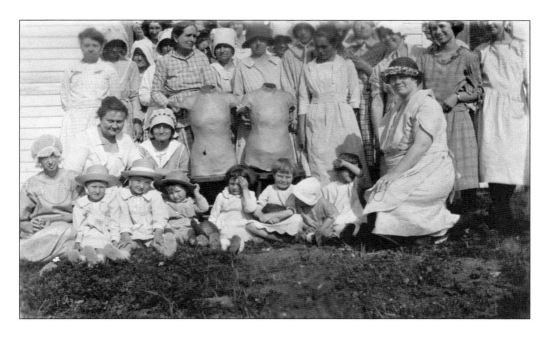

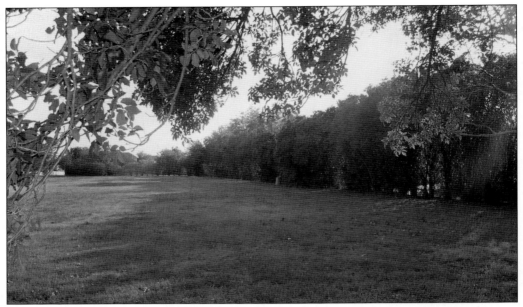

Presently, when looking south at the site, there is no trace of the school or church. Attendance at the Bethany Christian Church and Bethany School dwindled in the 1930s, as road improvements gave easier access to town. The buildings were eventually demolished due to lack of use. Today, all that remains of the Bethany site is the cemetery. The cemetery is located across the northern half of the rectangular historic site.

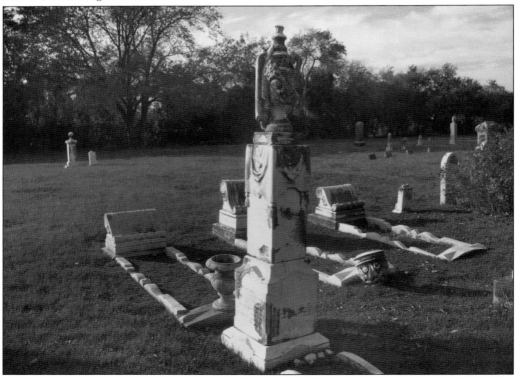

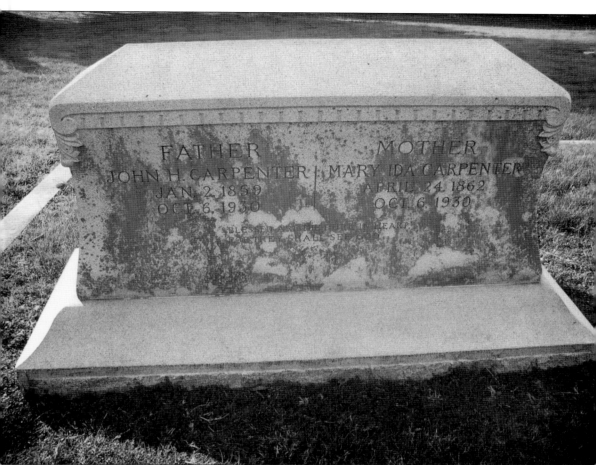

FATHER
JOHN H. CARPENTER
JAN. 2, 1859
OCT. 6, 1930

MOTHER
MARY IDA CARPENTER
APRIL 24, 1862
OCT. 6, 1930

John H. Carpenter was the son of Robert Washington "R.W." Carpenter. One of Plano's early settlers, R.W. ventured to Texas from Kentucky. John married Ida Coker; this is the couple's final resting place.

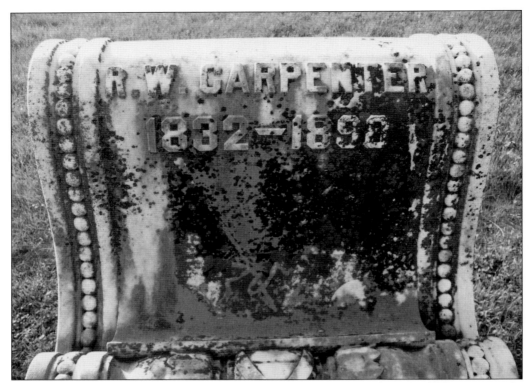

Besides being one of Plano's founding pioneers, R.W. Carpenter was also a Civil War veteran. As soon as the war started, Carpenter was quick to assemble a group of locals into a cavalry unit. The men in the unit elected him captain, a title he would keep until his death in 1898.

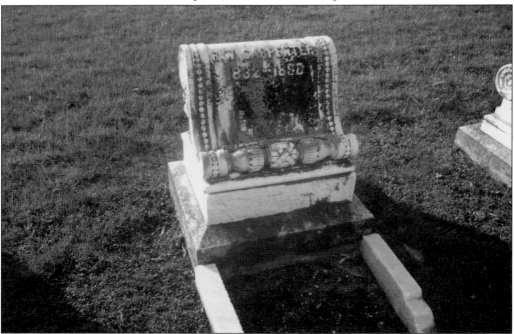

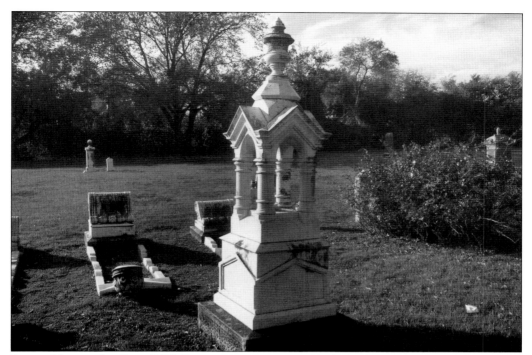

Pictured here is the Capt. R.W. Carpenter monument in Bethany Cemetery. Captain Carpenter is still recognized in Plano, as Carpenter Middle School is named after him. The school was built on land that was once the farm of Captain Carpenter's son Gip. Emma Kelly was the wife of Benjamin Owen Carpenter, John H. Carpenter's brother. Emma died at a very young age, and after her death, Benjamin Owen remarried, making Minnie Blanchford his wife.

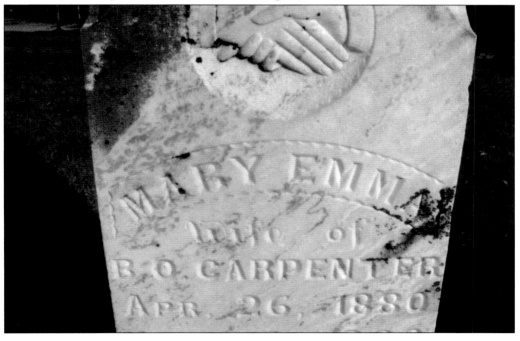

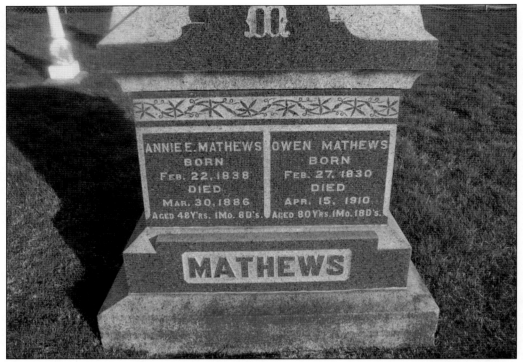

The Mathewses are another one of Plano's pioneer families. Owen Mathews was born in Louisville, Kentucky, and first visited Texas in 1848. He married Annie Elizabeth in 1853 and moved to Texas in 1856. He served in the Confederate army under Capt. R.W. Carpenter.

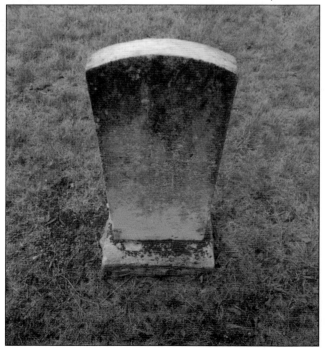

Pioneers sometimes had to use materials on hand for their beloved ones' tombstones. These stones were not always able to withstand Plano's extreme temperatures that range from over 100 degrees in the summer to freezing in winter. Also, the prairie wind caused these tombstones to deteriorate. This stone can no longer be read, as time and the weather have worn down the inscription. Now no one knows who is buried at this plot.

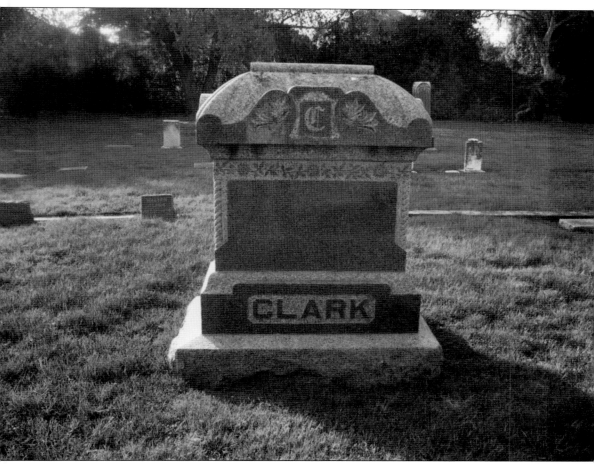

Seen here is the Clark family monument. The Clarks are another prominent Plano pioneer family. A Tennessee business and militiaman, Lanson Clark moved to Texas in 1845. He died from pneumonia in 1850, and his three orphan sons—Matt, Alvin, and Dick—were taken in by R.W. and Elizabeth Carpenter.

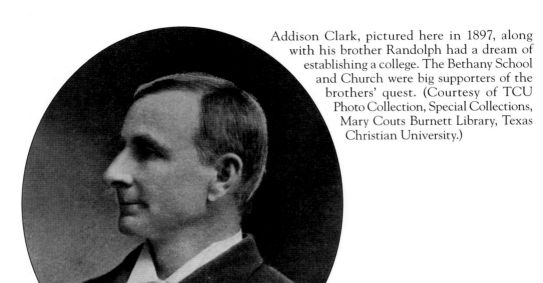

Addison Clark, pictured here in 1897, along with his brother Randolph had a dream of establishing a college. The Bethany School and Church were big supporters of the brothers' quest. (Courtesy of TCU Photo Collection, Special Collections, Mary Couts Burnett Library, Texas Christian University.)

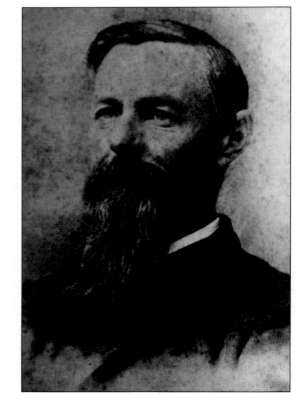

Randolph Clark, seen here in 1884, and Addison received loans from Plano pioneers Capt. R.W. Carpenter, C.S. Haggard, and Captain Bush. Randolph and Addison established Add-Ran College in 1869. Captain Carpenter and Captain Bush were repaid with land, and Haggard was repaid in scholarships. (Courtesy of TCU Photo Collection, Special Collections, Mary Couts Burnett Library, Texas Christian University.)

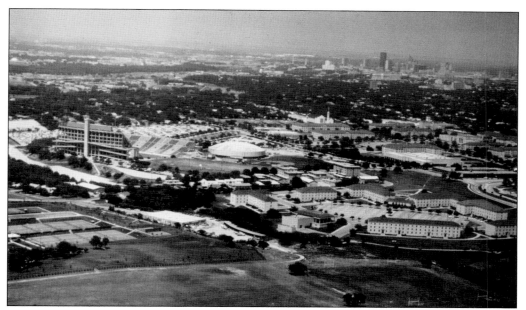

The little Add-Ran College would go through many changes, moving from Fort Worth to Thorp Spring to Waco and finally back to Fort Worth. In 1902, the name was changed to Texas Christian University. Seen here in a c. 1970 aerial view, it is now one of the major private universities in the state of Texas. (Courtesy of TCU Photo Collection, Special Collections, Mary Couts Burnett Library, Texas Christian University.)

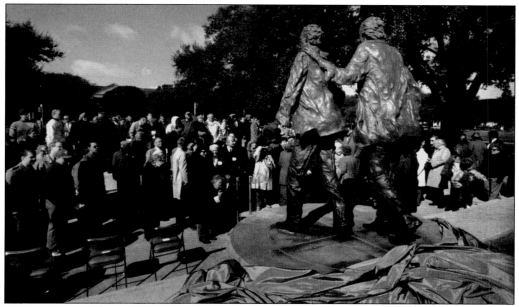

In 1993, Texas Christian University unveiled a statue of the Clark brothers. The statue is a great recognition of the university's founders. However, this leading Texas university might not even exist if it had not been for the support of Bethany Church and the Plano pioneers. (Courtesy of Linda Kaye Photo Collection, Special Collections Mary Couts Burnett Library, Texas Christian University.)

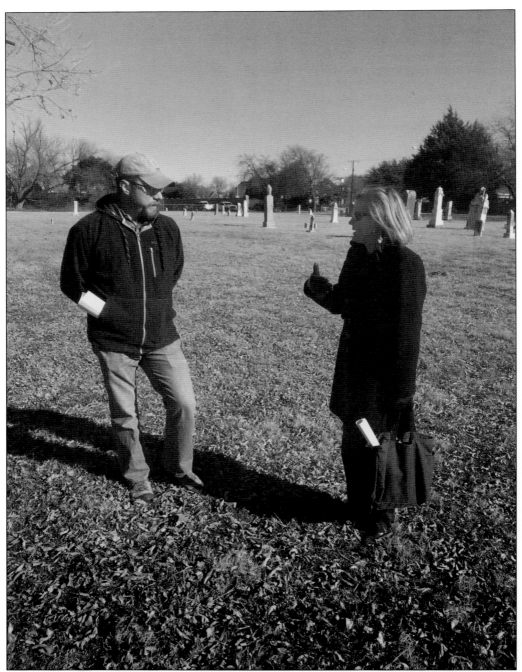

Dan Kieninger from Texas Cemetery Restoration and Candace Fountoulakis of the Plano Conservancy for Historic Preservation, Inc. meet on the Bethany site. The year 2014 brings a complete restoration of historic Bethany Cemetery. The restoration not only includes cleaning, leveling, and repair of the tombstones and monuments, but also a new entranceway, plantings, and landscaping.

Three

BOWMAN CEMETERY

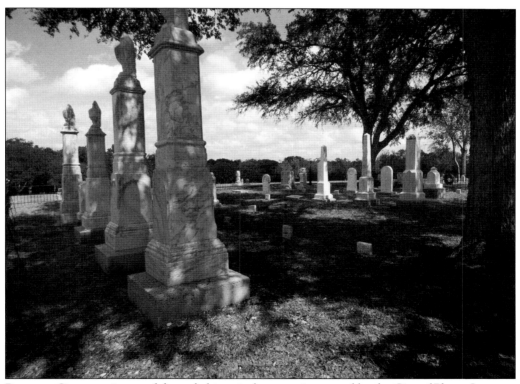

Bowman Cemetery is one of the only historical cemeteries owned by the City of Plano. It covers four acres and was deeded to the city after the death of Fannie Mae Bowman Adams in 1953. The rest of her land was sold and used to build subdivisions. The cemetery is surrounded by a park for the local residents.

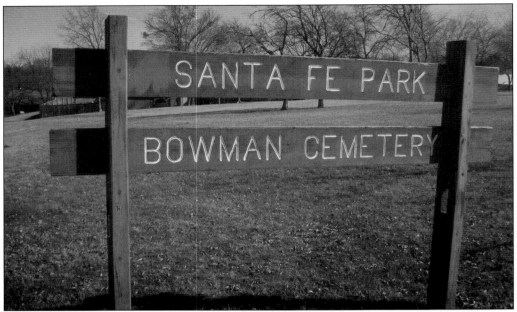

The cemetery land is located in Santa Fe Park of Plano, a green space for the residents of the local neighborhoods. The north side is an open field covering much of the park, and this is where one can find wildflowers blooming profusely in the spring. The records of the burials outside of the fenced family plots are sometimes documented, but many are left to their oral histories. It is said and understood that both black and white burials took place at Bowman Cemetery. It is believed that the burial plots of the slaves in the area are where the wildflowers bloom.

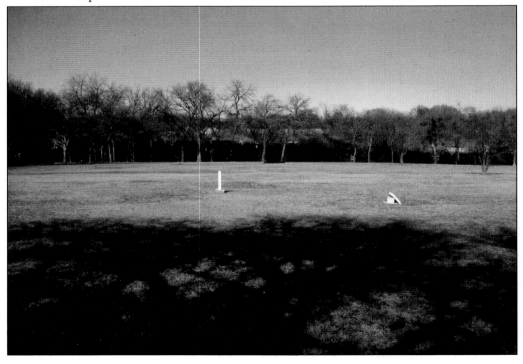

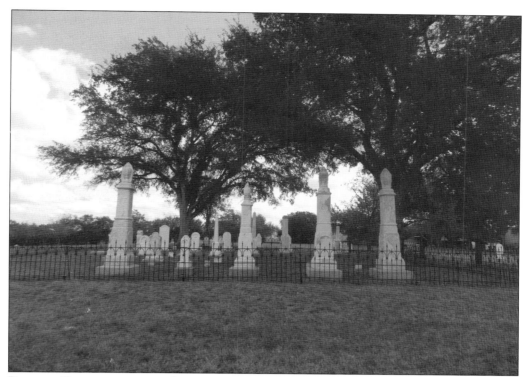

Bowman Cemetery was created when a fatal illness struck John Davis Bowman's daughter Julia Anna Bowman Russell, and he utilized space on his brother's land to create a burial site that would eventually become known as Bowman Cemetery. Julia became sick and passed away quickly upon the family's arrival to Texas. Since they were new to the area, they were not able to follow any geographically established burial traditions. Due to this, the family broke down one of the wagons they were using for their move and made a coffin for Julia out of it. The Bowman brothers became prominent members of the Plano area, investing time and money into development. The Bowman and the Brown families traveled to Texas together, and that is why their family plots are located next to each other in this historic cemetery. The first wave of migration to the area was from 1845 to 1846 and brought 822 colonists. Pictured here is the Bowman family section.

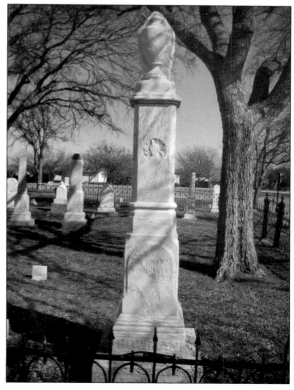

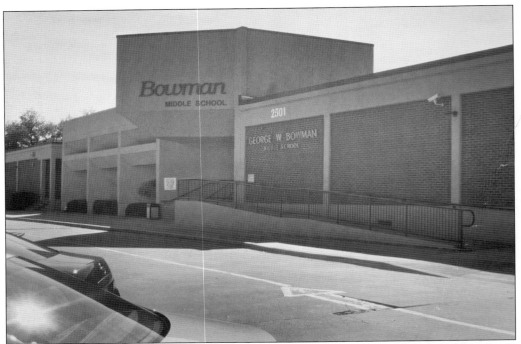

Bowman Middle School, named in George W. Bowman's honor, is one of the 13 middle schools serving Plano Independent School District. The middle school was built in 1976.

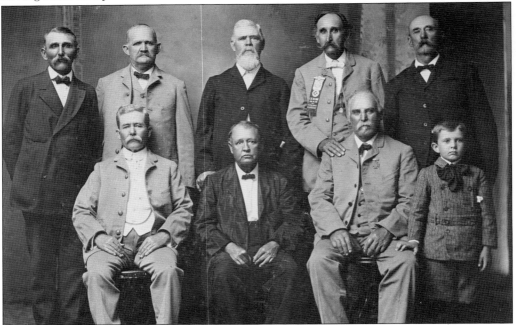

George W. Bowman (second row, second from left) would become one of the most prominent of the settlers buried in this cemetery. He became president of the Plano National Bank shortly after its founding. He was a director of the Texas Electric Railway company and served on the Plano School Board (pictured) for 10 years.

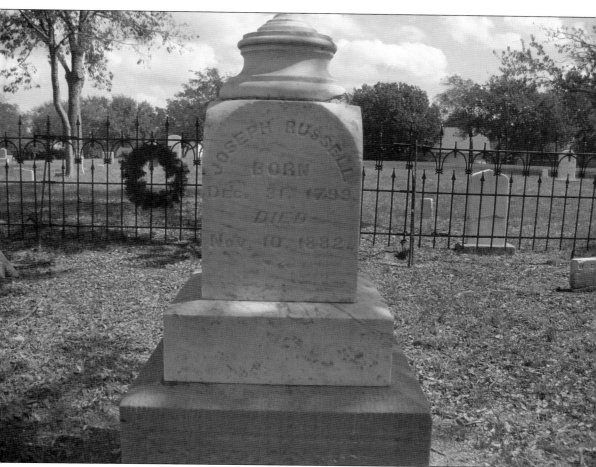

Joseph Russell came to Texas in 1845 with his wife, Elizabeth Grey. They organized one of the first Methodist churches in the county, which met in their home until 1856. This church would eventually have four internationally traveling missionaries. Joseph Russell arrived early enough to be considered one of the early Peters Colonists. When he and Elizabeth moved to Texas, they already had five children who made the journey with them. The Russell family also travelled with the Browns and the Bowmans during their southern migration. Pictured here is Joseph's tombstone.

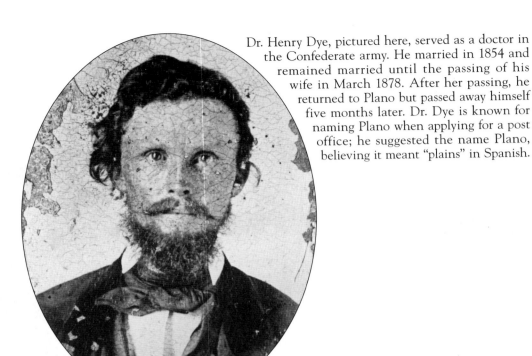

Dr. Henry Dye, pictured here, served as a doctor in the Confederate army. He married in 1854 and remained married until the passing of his wife in March 1878. After her passing, he returned to Plano but passed away himself five months later. Dr. Dye is known for naming Plano when applying for a post office; he suggested the name Plano, believing it meant "plains" in Spanish.

Dr. Henry Dye was an innovative surgeon. He is known for keeping an incredibly detailed medical journal during his time as a Civil War doctor. The journal is on loan to Duke University, and new historical works continue to be published based on its information. Pictured here is Dr. Dye's tombstone.

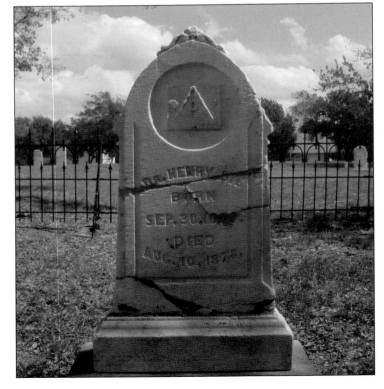

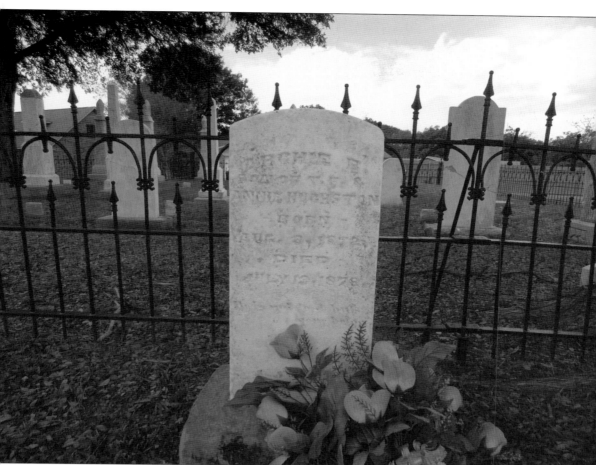

Archie Hughston came to Plano at 19 years old in 1892 from Alabama. He and his brother Thomas Lee Hughston opened a grocery store. However, after six months of operation, the fire of March 25, 1893, destroyed the grocery store. Due to this, Archie accepted a position as manager at the newly built corn-sheller and elevator. Eventually, Archie and his brother bought the grain company and named it the Hughston Brothers Grain Company. The company is listed in one of the first local phone directories, published in 1908.

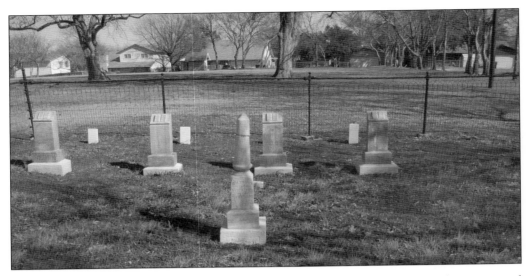

The Brown family has its own section in a secondary plot. Robert Brown, a Peters Colonist, married Elizabeth Russell. This union was one of the many connections between the Bowmans, Browns, and Russells, as they were the best of family friends. On January 2, 1850, Elizabeth and Robert had a son named George Pearis Brown. He was the first school principal in the area, a county attorney, and eventually an assistant US district attorney. He would retire to a private law practice. George P. is an integral part of Plano history because, in the 1930s, he collected oral histories, which were turned into 300 pages of county heritage endearingly called the "Brown Papers."

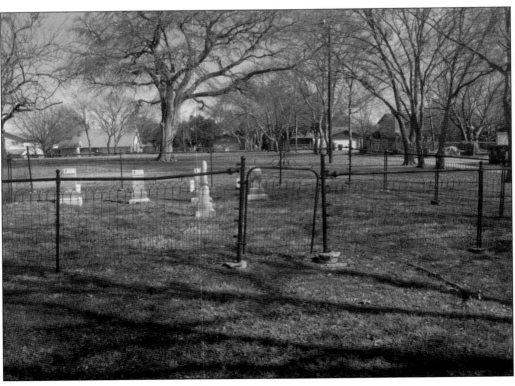

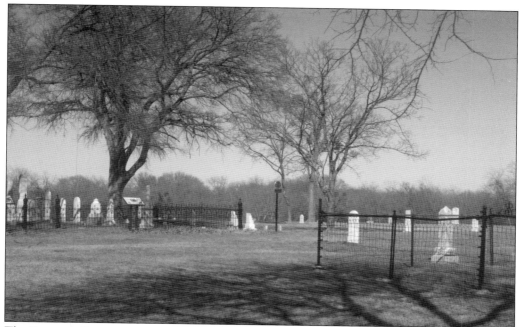

The Bowman Cemetery is currently 145 years old. The park upkeep is primarily maintained by the City of Plano in connection with its association. This means that the cemetery is also protected and maintained to a small degree by the city. The Plano Conservancy for Historic Preservation, Inc. took on the task of restoring the cemetery, as well as registering the cemetery with a Historic Texas Cemetery Medallion. Two members of the Boy Scouts of America have earned their Eagle Scout status by completing community-based projects that involved repairing the cemetery fences. Repairing a historic cemetery is a large task with multiple steps.

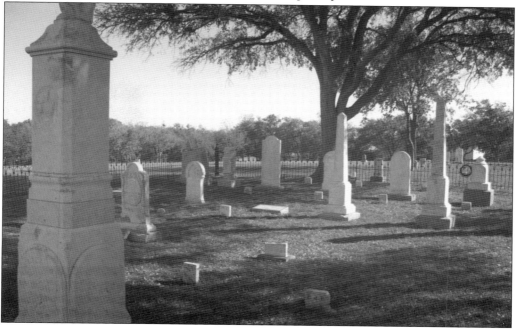

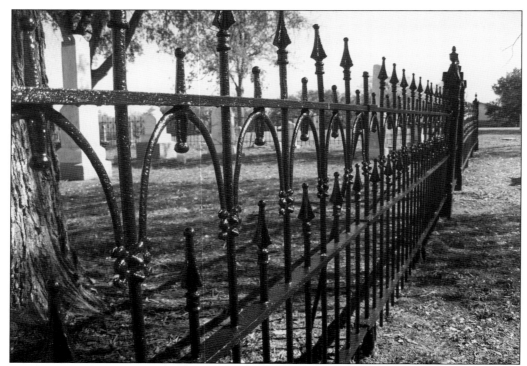

The Plano Conservancy for Historic Preservation, Inc. first needed to test the paint on the fence to see if it was lead-based. It is always the intention during a renovation to use the same materials originally used when it is environmentally safe. Fortunately, the company hired to do this testing did not find any lead-based paint on the fence, and priming and painting was allowed to move forward.

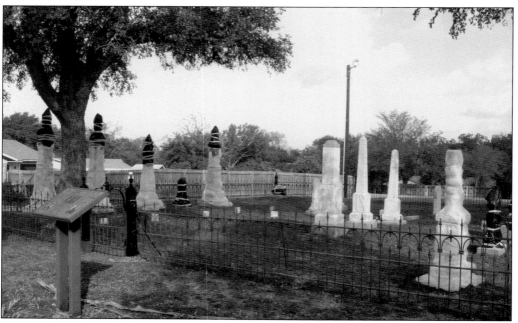

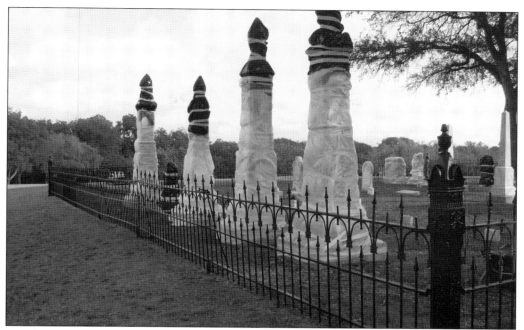

It is also important to hire an expert at headstone cleaning and repair, as typical cleaning solvents can be dangerous to the historical headstones and the ground surrounding them. An expert is carefully trained on what tools to use in order to move headstones and how to be respectful during the restoration process. When working in a cemetery, it is always important to be respectful of the families and people buried there, as well as respectful to the people who have the cemetery as a neighbor.

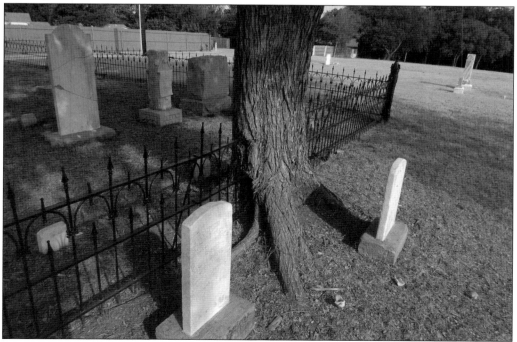

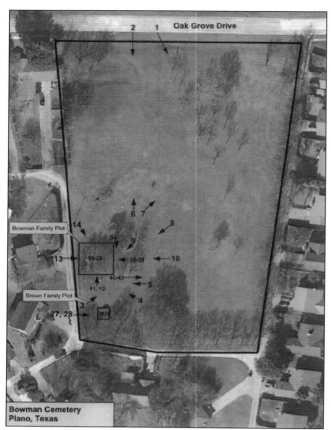

Bowman Cemetery
Plano, Texas

Not everyone chooses to live next to a cemetery; however, when developers take the time to incorporate a historic cemetery tastefully into the housing around it, the community usually becomes very protective and respectful to the families honored there. *Dallas Morning News* reporter Thaai Walker covered the restoration and quotes John Dooley, one of the Scouts: "It really looks good, and now that we've finished it I think it shows respect to the people buried there."

One of the Troop 181 Boy Scouts, John Lance used the opportunity of Bowman's Cemetery restoration for his Eagle Scout project. Repainting of the original wrought iron fence at Bowman Cemetery would be a historic preservation project that met his Eagle Scout requirements and left a lasting historical impact on the cemetery.

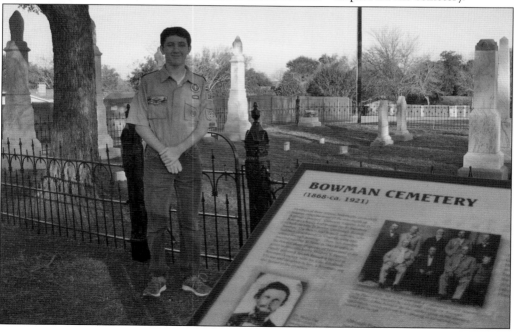

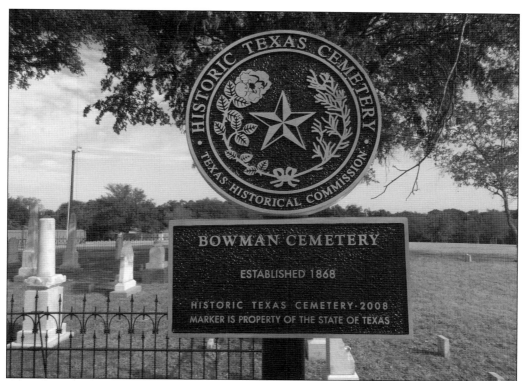

After the completion of the restoration of the fences and headstones, the Collin County Master Gardeners planted irises, as well as horse herb, an ivy ground cover. They oversaw the scattering of buffalo grass seed to further enrich and protect the grounds of the cemetery. One of the overseers and coordinators of the project, Candance Fountoulakis, is quoted in a *Dallas Morning News* story: "a very satisfying component of the cooperative effort was the partnership of so many different groups to achieve a successful outcome."

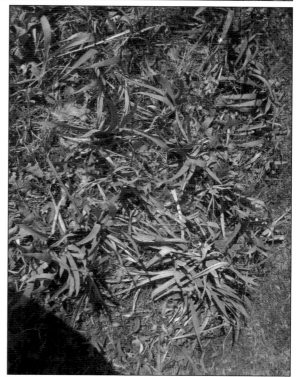

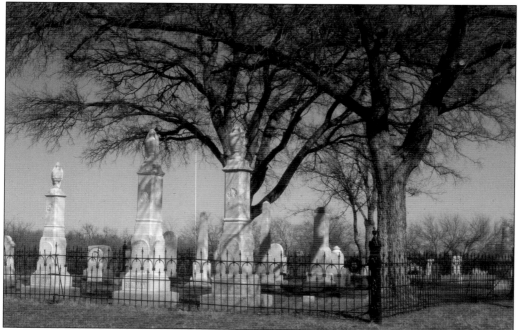

Fountoulakis continues by stating that the "combined talents of historic preservationists, the City of Plano, and the Boy Scouts of America have created a model that can be employed at other pioneer cemeteries within the community." Bringing a community together on a project is tough work and requires dedicated leadership. These leaders met with homeowners, youth activity groups, city officials, and other organizations to create a multifaceted effort of different skills. The Plano Conservancy for Historic Preservation, Inc. has dedicated itself and shaped its mission statement around the pursuit of preserving these historic pioneer cemeteries.

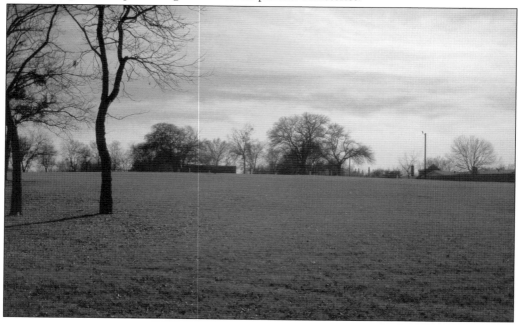

Four

ROUTH CEMETERY

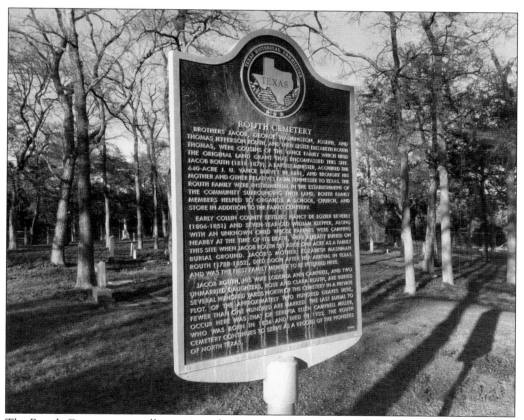

The Routh Cemetery actually consists of two cemeteries—the small Routh Family Cemetery and the larger Routh Cemetery. The Routh Family Cemetery is the final resting place of Jacob Routh, his wife, daughters, and their pets. The main Routh Cemetery contains about 200 graves, with the Campbells being one of the prominent families buried there. About 100 of the graves in this cemetery are unmarked. Jacob bought the land in 1852.

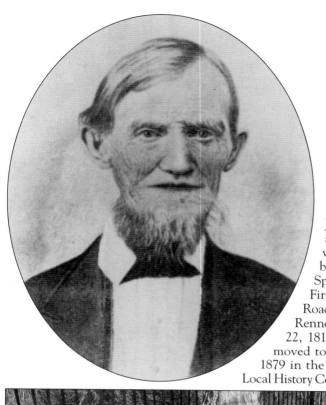

Jacob Routh was a Baptist preacher at Spring Creek Baptist Church, which was on the same property but further east near Plano Road. Spring Creek Baptist Church became First Baptist Church of Plano. Plano Road was once a stagecoach run, as was Renner Road. Routh was born December 22, 1818, in Dandridge, Tennessee, and moved to Texas in 1851. He died April 30, 1879 in the Plano area. (Left, courtesy of the Local History Collection, Richardson Public Library.)

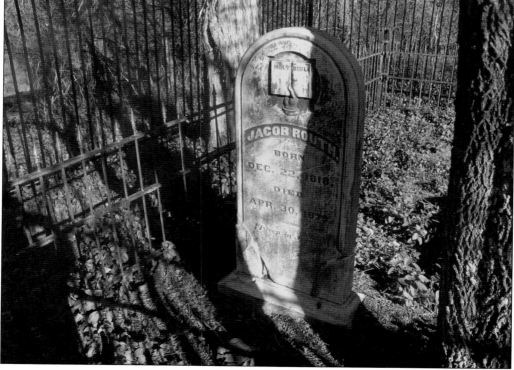

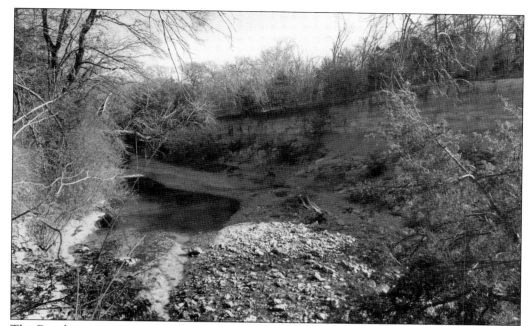

The Routh property is now contained inside the Spring Creek Nature Center. Spring Creek runs through the middle of the site. The Routh Family Cemetery is located just beyond the creek's cliff. The site is about two miles south of downtown Plano and is now a part of the city of Richardson.

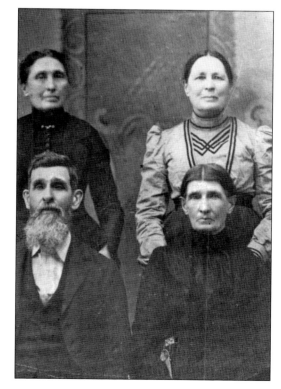

Lodemia Ann Campbell Routh is pictured with members of her family: Serepta Ellen Campbell Routh, William Lafayette Campbell, and Margaret Emma Campbell Stanley. Lodemia married Jacob Routh on October 30, 1853. Her father is Robert Fleming Campbell. (Courtesy of the Local History Collection, Richardson Public Library.)

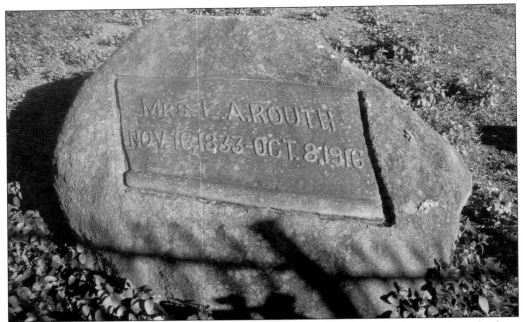

The Lodemia Ann Campbell Routh gravesite has a unique marker, a large stone brought from Colorado with her name, birth date, and date of death carved in the side. It is located next to that of her husband, Jacob Routh. Their daughters Rose and Clara are buried beside them. Clara's plot is the final marked burial in the Routh Family Cemetery.

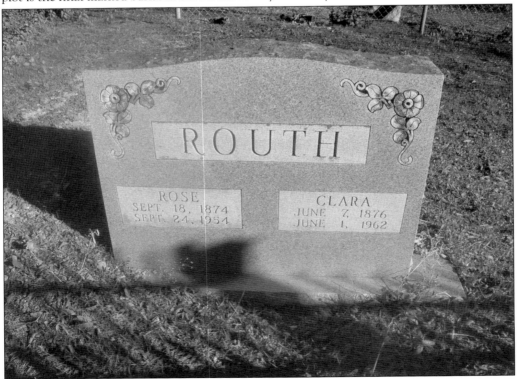

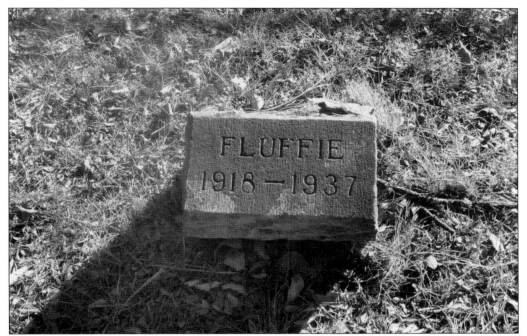

Clara Routh had three dogs—Sharon, Rinnett, and Theda. The Rouths loved their animals and felt that it was important that they all have grave markers. Fluffie the cat lived a very long life (19 years). Fluffie belonged to Aunt Clara Routh. Fluffie's gravesite is adjacent to the three dogs'.

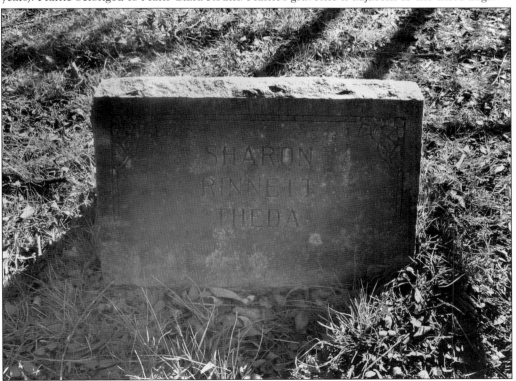

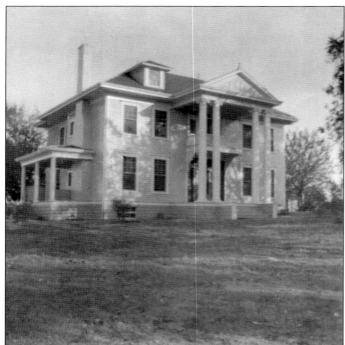

Jacob Routh started building his home in 1860. The two-story house with four statuesque Greek columns was not finished until 1871. The delay in construction was due to the outbreak of the Civil War and the struggles of Reconstruction. Unfortunately, the Routh home has been lost to history. In 1965, the house was the victim of vandalism and arson. The home was located on Renner Road in present-day Richardson. (Courtesy of the Local History Collection, Richardson Public Library.)

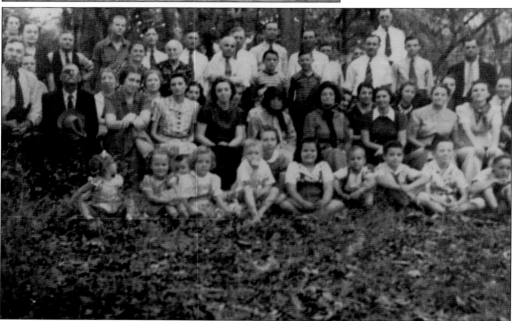

This is a picture of the 1938 Routh family reunion at the Routh homesite just south of Plano. Routh family members include Vivian S. Barron, Madge Carver Barron, Cecil Thornton Barron, Stanley J. Jr. Mendenhall, Stanley J. Mendenhall, Stanton J. Barron, Haskel Roach, Jake Barron or Jimmy Rogers, Robert Webb, Roy Patton Howell, John M. Campbell, Rosa Routh, Clara Routh, Virginia Roach, Mildred C. Rogers, Julia Mendenhall, Florence Rogers, Mary Ann Coit, and Louise Rogers. (Courtesy of the Local History Collection, Richardson Public Library.)

Family Bibles were a common way to document important events in a family's history. These two pages are from the Thomas-Routh family Bible. Family Bibles are usually handed down through the years with the passing of generations. Each successive generation records the family's births, deaths, and other important events. Some of these family Bibles also include photographs, letters, and articles clipped from newspapers. These pages show the birth dates and dates of death of members of the Thomas family. Today, these old family Bibles are excellent resources for people researching their genealogy. (Both, courtesy of the Local History Collection, Richardson Public Library.)

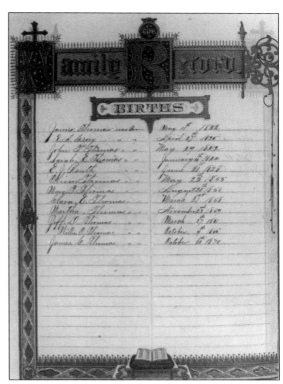

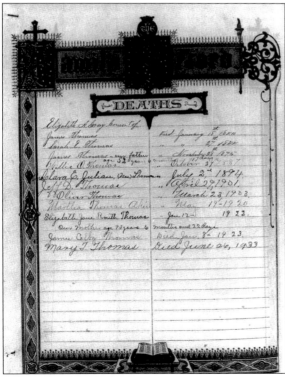

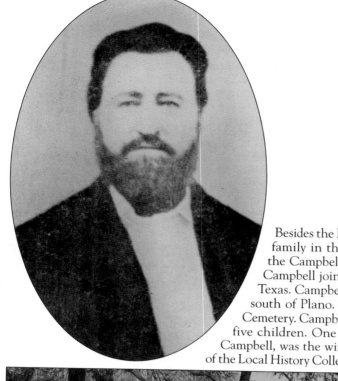

Besides the Routh family, the other prominent family in this area of the Texas frontier was the Campbell family. In 1851, Robert Fleming Campbell joined Jacob Routh on his journey to Texas. Campbell paid $2 an acre for his land just south of Plano. He is buried in the main Routh Cemetery. Campbell was married twice and fathered five children. One of his daughters, Lodemia Ann Campbell, was the wife of Jacob Routh. (Left, courtesy of the Local History Collection, Richardson Public Library.)

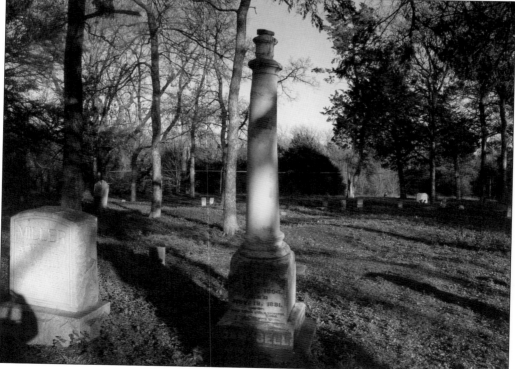

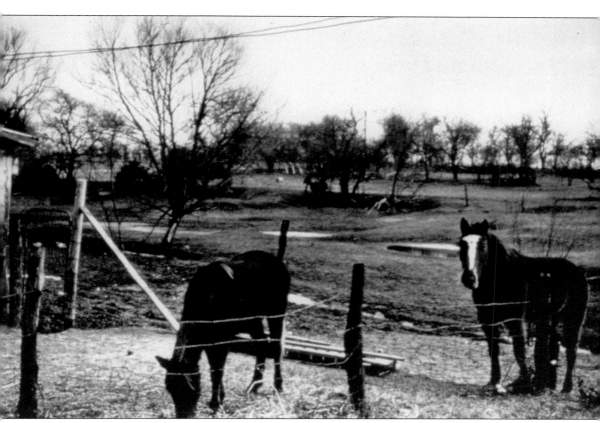

The original Robert Fleming Campbell farm was in the area of Campbell Road and Prairie Creek Drive. The land that Campbell bought for $2 an acre would sell in the range of $100,000 an acre in 2012. (Courtesy of the Local History Collection, Richardson Public Library.)

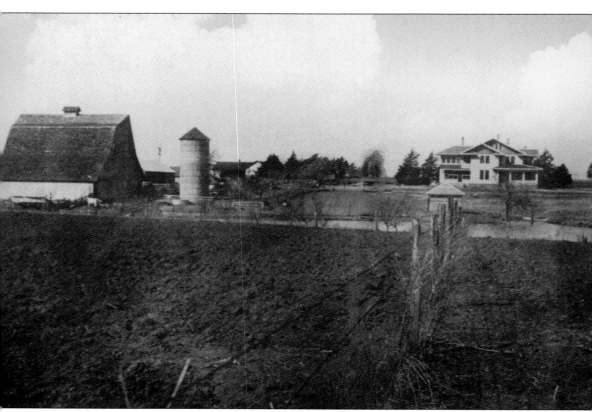

Robert Fleming Campbell's son John Meade Campbell established this farm. The site included the John Meade Campbell home, a barn, silo, and a pond. John Meade passed away in McKinney, Texas, in 1954. (Courtesy of the Local History Collection, Richardson Public Library.)

James White "J.W." Campbell was the son of Robert Fleming Campbell. He was born in Jefferson County, Tennessee, and came to Texas with his father. He is buried close to his father's grave. The last burial in Routh Cemetery was conducted in 1922. Serepta Ellen Campbell Routh Miller, daughter of Robert Fleming Campbell, died on May 8, 1922. She is buried close to her father.

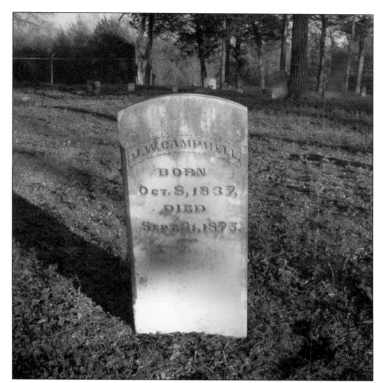

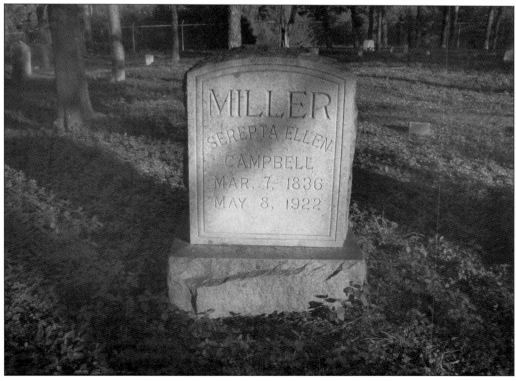

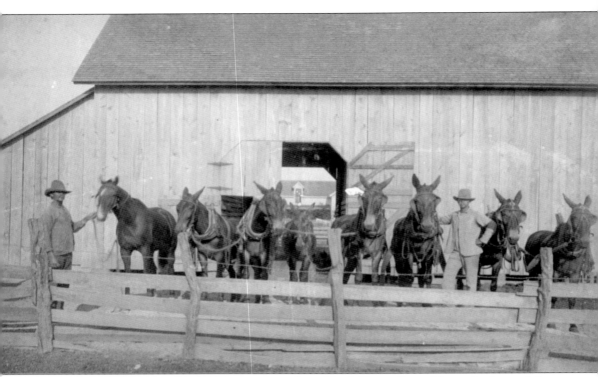

The Campbell clan became well known throughout North Texas. One of the main thoroughfares in Richardson—Campbell Road—bears their name. Pictured is the E.O. Campbell farm in Richardson, Texas. Ben Coldwell and Jim W. Campbell show off their mules. The Plano/Richardson area was once known throughout the United States for raising mules. For a working farm, mules were sturdier than horses and better suited for the Texas heat. (Courtesy of the Local History Collection, Richardson Public Library.)

Five

PLANO MUTUAL CEMETERY

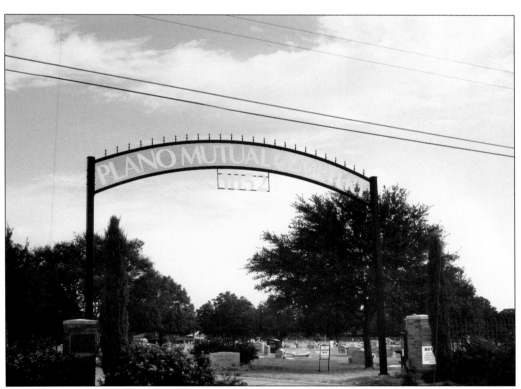

A modern cemetery with a storied past, Plano Mutual has a Texas Historical Marker and represents several founding families of Plano. Peters Colonists from the Bowman, Forman, and Rice families gave land from adjoining properties to form the original cemetery boundaries. In 1997, there were 20 schools named after people buried in Plano Mutual.

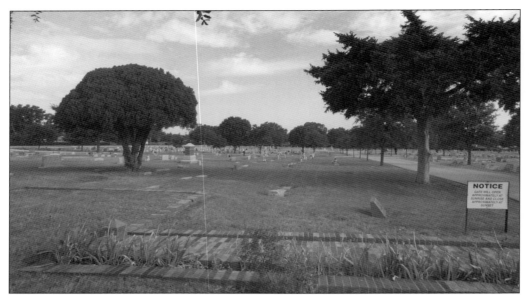

The first person buried in this cemetery was a Dr. Lillie, from Kentucky. He rode horseback from Kentucky to Texas, and due to the exposure from the travel, he fell ill with pneumonia and died not long after his arrival. Dr. Lillie's grave is unmarked, and therefore, the exact spot is undetermined. However, the second burial was that of Eleanor Hawkins and her marker is still legible, stating she passed away and was buried in 1853. Hawkins had traveled to Texas to be a teacher and passed away at 16.

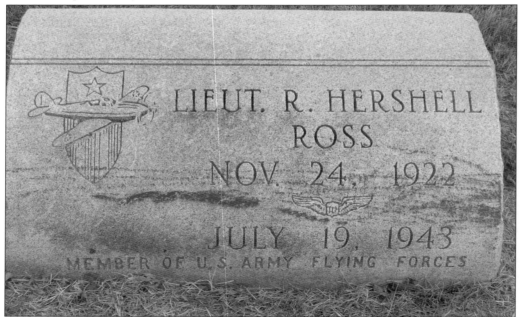

Over 100 years later, Plano Mutual is still an active cemetery, and it is rare in that it continues to allow upright monuments. Many veterans have made Plano Mutual their final resting place, with their surviving family using the upright monuments as a way of honoring these veterans for many years.

The Forman area was marked by a large *Maclura pomifera*, or horse apple tree. This area is still used for Forman family burials. There is a standing oral history of a horse thief being hanged from this tree and then buried in an unmarked grave in the area.

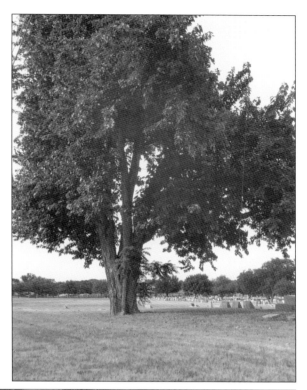

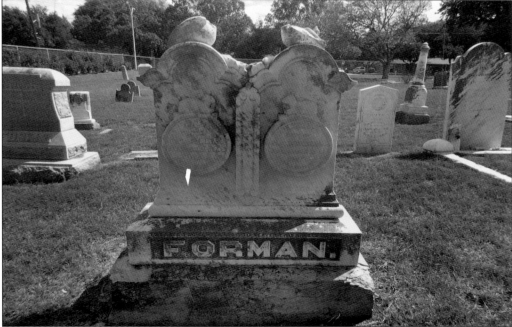

William Forman came from Kentucky in 1846 with his two sons. They officially took residence in Collin County in 1850. Forman purchased a large tract of land and put it to very good use. Eventually, he used the land to build a gristmill, a distillery, a cooperage, and a sawmill.

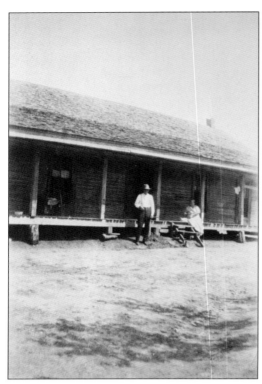

Forman also ran a post office from his home until 1851, when he successfully petitioned for an official post office to be established. In order for a post office to be established, the town had to have official boundaries and an official name. He and Henry Dye named the area Plano, and Forman was recognized as the first postmaster. He died in 1856, and Forman Elementary is named after him. Pictured at left is the Forman home, and below is the grave marker of his wife.

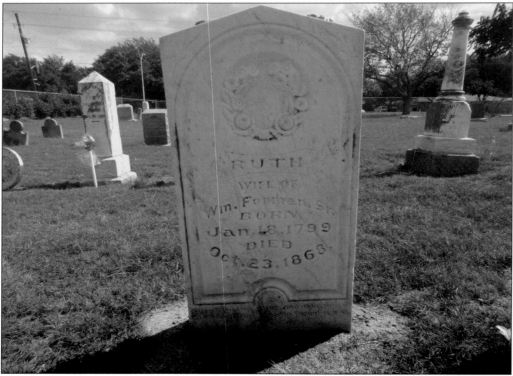

Olney Davis was born in Waxahachie. When he was a young man, he left for Illinois for college. After graduating from the University of Illinois, Davis returned to Plano and worked his father's land. He had nine children with his wife, Effie Susan Mathews. Davis was on the original board of directors for Plano National Bank in 1887 and served as its vice president for several years. He was named the first president of the Plano School Board in 1899. Davis Elementary is named in his honor. The Odd Fellows Lodge No. 114 had a designated section in Plano Mutual Cemetery. Pictured here is Olney in his Odd Fellows uniform.

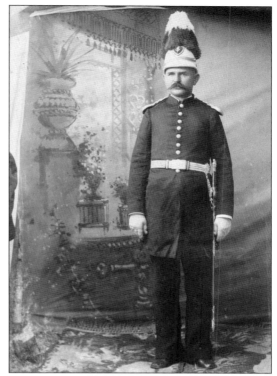

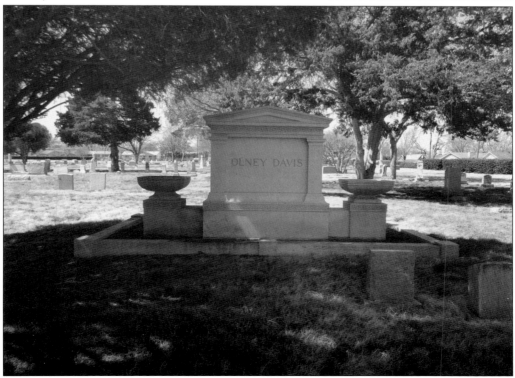

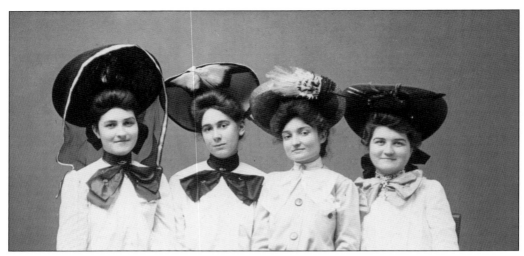

In 1888, the Davises moved into town. Olney Davis was instrumental in organizing the Plano Lumber Company; he served as mayor for two terms and was a town alderman. Davis was honored with being named president of the Texas Ginners Association. He and his wife, Effie, were members of the First Christian Church. They had nine children, three of whom died in infancy or early childhood. Pictured here are Effie Davis (left) and the Davis girls (above).

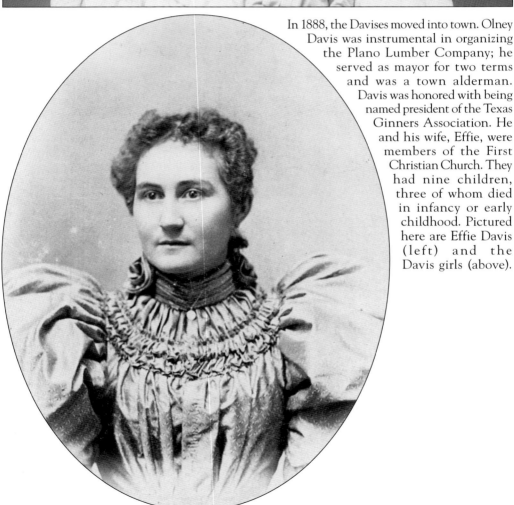

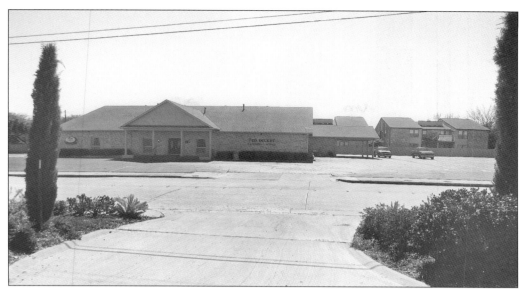

Andrew Wetsel, the area's first undertaker, is also buried in Plano Mutual Cemetery. He was famous locally for his carpentry skills and furniture making. Wealthier residents began requesting that Wetsel make coffins for their loved ones. Eventually, it became quite a business for him, and he and E.O. Harrington founded the funeral home that is now known as Ted Dickey Funeral Home. E.O. had seven siblings. His parents were from Kentucky, and his father was awarded 320 acres upon settling in Peters Colony. During the 1850s, E.O.'s parents were some of the leading landowners. Eventually, E.O.'s son Ted Harrington would join them in the funeral business. Mrs. Harvey Angel told a story where she was to hold the lantern while E.O. and Ted were embalming a local man in 1926. Pictured below is the Harrington section at Plano Mutual.

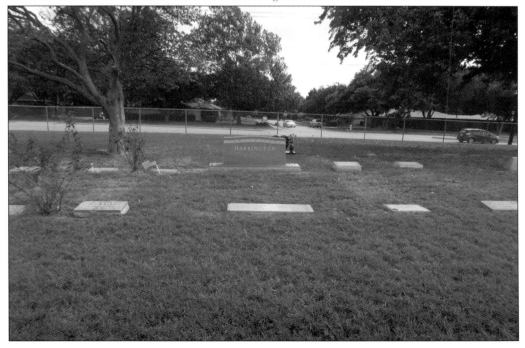

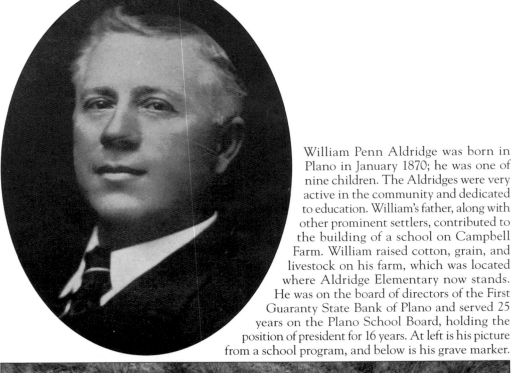

William Penn Aldridge was born in Plano in January 1870; he was one of nine children. The Aldridges were very active in the community and dedicated to education. William's father, along with other prominent settlers, contributed to the building of a school on Campbell Farm. William raised cotton, grain, and livestock on his farm, which was located where Aldridge Elementary now stands. He was on the board of directors of the First Guaranty State Bank of Plano and served 25 years on the Plano School Board, holding the position of president for 16 years. At left is his picture from a school program, and below is his grave marker.

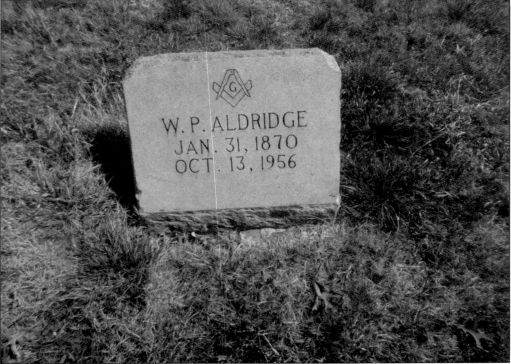

W. P. ALDRIDGE
JAN. 31, 1870
OCT. 13, 1956

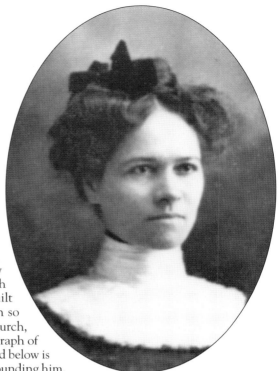

Jeremiah Boggess worked during the Civil War as an engineer for troops and supply trains. When the war was over, he moved with his wife and four children to Plano. He built a log cabin farmhouse and a house in town so that his children could be close to school, church, and social activities. To the right is a photograph of Jeremiah's daughter Dru Boggess, and pictured below is his grave marker and those of his family surrounding him.

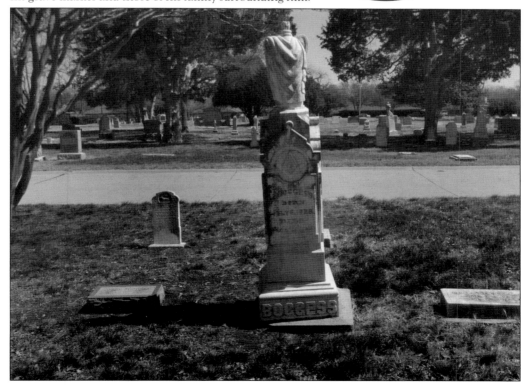

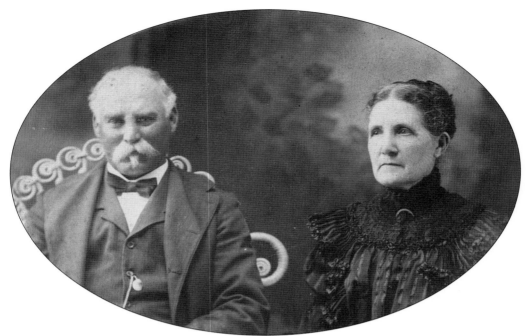

F.M. Armstrong enlisted in the Confederate army at 19 and was a member of McKenzie's Raiders, a fierce group of fighters famous for their courage and dedication. Armstrong was quoted as saying, "We were not whipped—we were just overpowered," when recollecting the lack of ammunition and supplies. After the war, his work took him to Texas, and eventually he relocated and started a family in Plano. A successful cotton and corn farmer, Armstrong was a longtime member of the Plano Masonic Lodge, and after his passing on February 17, 1933, he was buried in Plano Mutual under the sponsorship of the Masonic lodge. Above is a picture of Armstrong and his wife, and below is his grave marker.

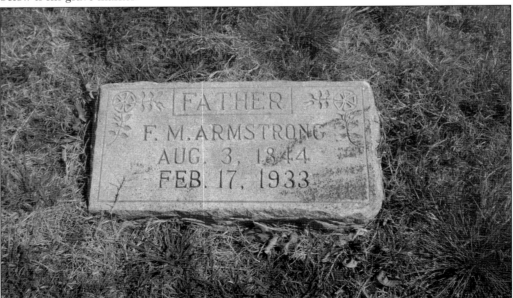

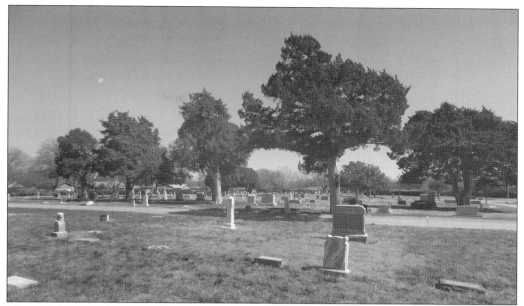

Many of the early doctors of the area are buried in Plano Mutual, and one is Dr. Rip Wilson. Dr. Wilson was known as quite a character and would say exactly what he thought. He is recorded in the census as caring for a wounded man with a bad reputation. Another man in the area asked, "Doctor, is he very bad hurt? Is it serious?" Dr. Wilson looked up and replied, "I'm afraid not."

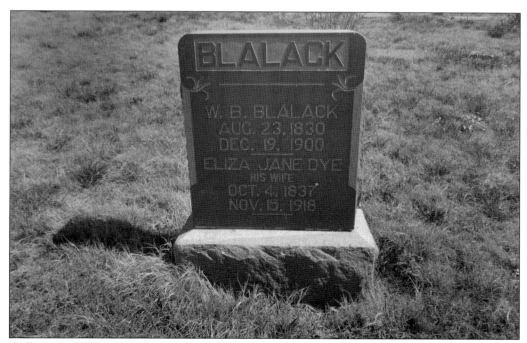

William B. "W.B." Blalock was named Plano postmaster on December 24, 1856. Also in 1856, Blalock rented a space from Eli Murphy and ran a grocery store with his brother Thomas. They had only arrived in Plano in 1854 but were officially settled by 1856.

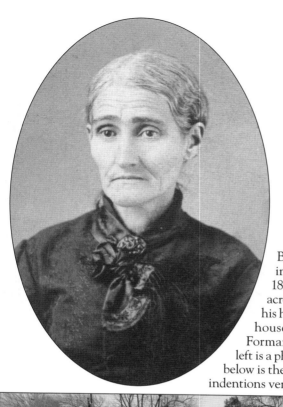

Benjamin Franklin "B.F." Mathews was born in Kentucky and married Mary Ann Yager in 1846. They moved to Plano and farmed 640 acres. B.F. was a very skilled carpenter, building his home on Spring Creek and then constructing houses for others in the area, including Joe Forman, whose home still stands today. To the left is a photograph of B.F.'s wife, Mary Ann. Pictured below is their joint monument. Exposure has made the indentions very hard to read without the proper sunlight.

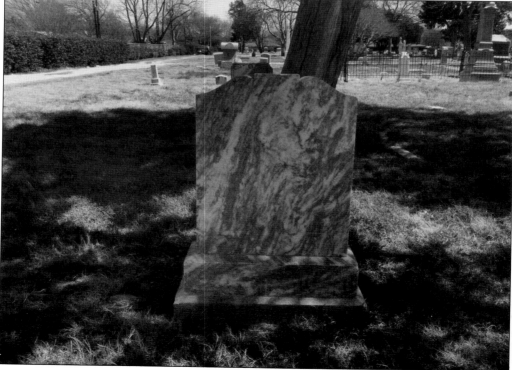

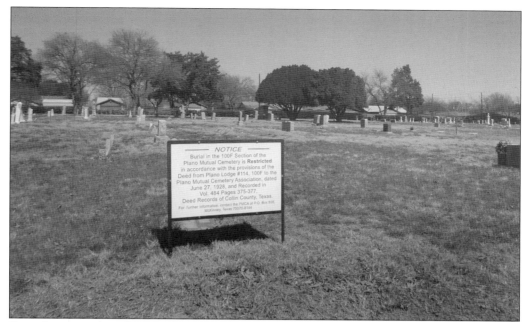

Over the years, there have been certain sections allotted for local groups. One of these sections is for Freemason Lodge No. 768. This section is still designated for this local chapter and is maintained currently by its members. In 1993, the lodge donated an obelisk to mark and honor the designated section. The Plano area has a rich tradition of Freemasons. Many corner markers in the historic district denote the work of Freemasons and their dedication to building and preserving the town of Plano.

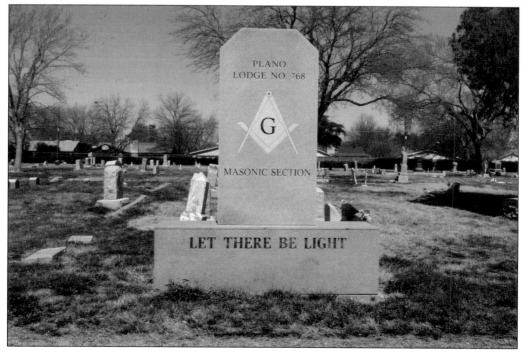

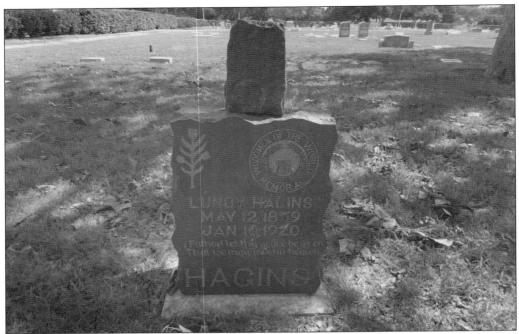

Two other designated sections were for the Knights of Pythias Lodge No. 39, which was sold a year after its designation, and the Woodmen of the World Camp No. 742. Pictured here are the two monument styles traditionally used by Woodmen of the World; one of the styles is with the traditional seal and marker, and another monument style resembles the stump or trunk of a tree. These sections are also occupied by families of group members. Eventually, both sections returned to the ownership of the cemetery and were used until new sections of the cemetery were opened.

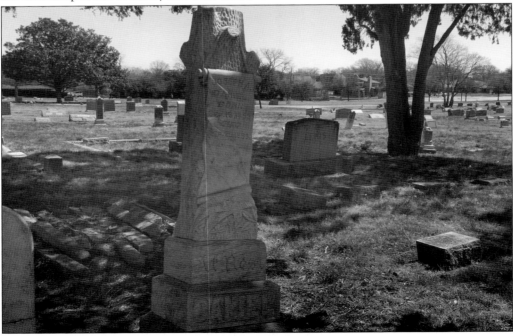

Six

ROWLETT CREEK CEMETERY

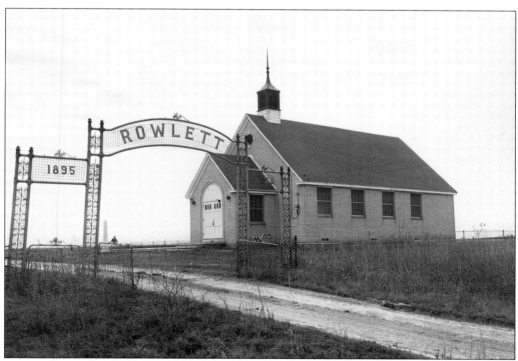

Rowlett Creek Cemetery, with its chapel still intact, is home to numerous Plano pioneer families. A visitor to this cemetery will recognize family names etched in tombstones and given to Plano's streets, parks, and schools. The cemetery is located northwest of downtown Plano.

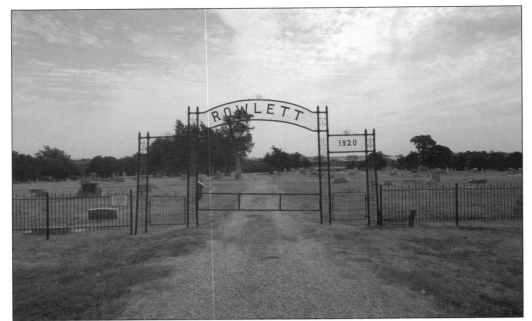

Pictured is the entrance to Rowlett Creek Cemetery. The cemetery is maintained by the Rowlett Creek Cemetery Association. Dr. Daniel Rowlett left Kentucky and came to Texas in 1836 with his wife and six other families. Rowlett settled in the area of what is today Bonham, Texas. He located much of an 1838 land grant in the fertile ground along the tributary that would soon bear his name—Rowlett Creek.

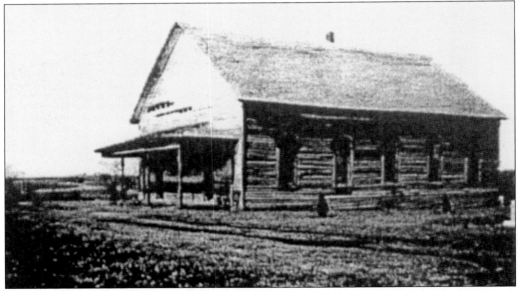

After meeting in homes and outdoors, seven charter members organized the Wilson Creek Church of United Baptists in 1848, under the leadership of Rev. David Myers. In 1852, the church name was changed to Rowlett Creek Baptist Church. It is believed to be the oldest Baptist church in Collin County. Three of the original church ministers are laid to rest in the cemetery—J.C. Portman, C.E. Morgan, and C.A. Stanton.

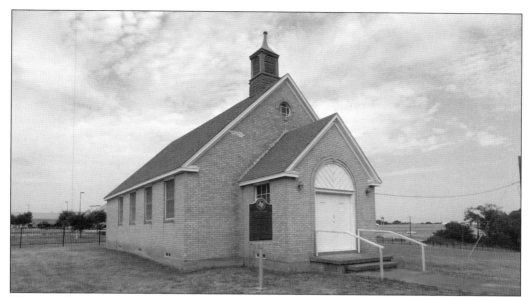

The chapel was remodeled in 1950. The present church stands abandoned, without a congregation today. A Texas Historical Marker tells the story of the site's history. In the state of Texas, sponsors may apply for official historical markers through their local county historical commissions. The purpose of the Texas Historical Markers is to educate the public on a specific piece of Texas history. An application must meet certain requirements to be approved by the Texas Historical Commission to qualify for a marker.

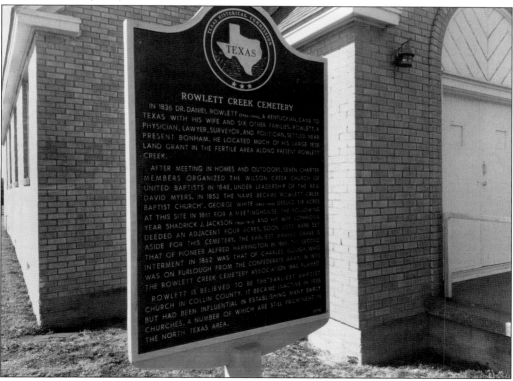

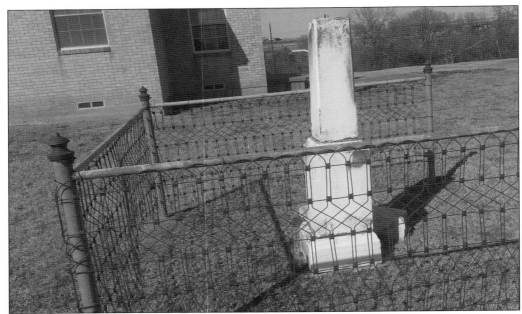

This is the monument for George White. White donated a section of the land for Rowlett Creek Cemetery. He was a surveyor, laying out the plat for Rowlett Creek Cemetery. White also platted Pecan Grove Memorial Park in McKinney, just north of Plano. In 1861, he deeded six acres at the site for a meetinghouse. In 1862, Shadrick J. Jackson and his wife, Sophronia, deeded an adjacent four acres. Soon, lots were set aside for this cemetery. White is buried in Pecan Grove Cemetery. He was also a private in the Confederate army and served in the Texas Cavalry.

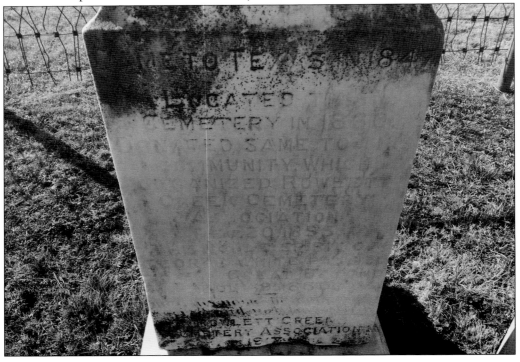

The 36th president of the United States, Lyndon Baines Johnson (LBJ), is a native Texan, born in Stonewall. President Johnson's ancestry can be traced to Plano, Texas. Many of his ancestors lived in the Plano area, and some are buried in Plano.

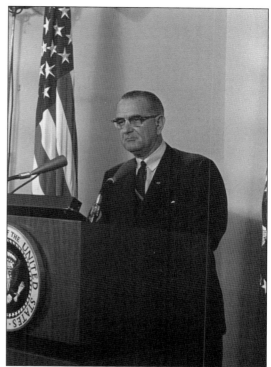

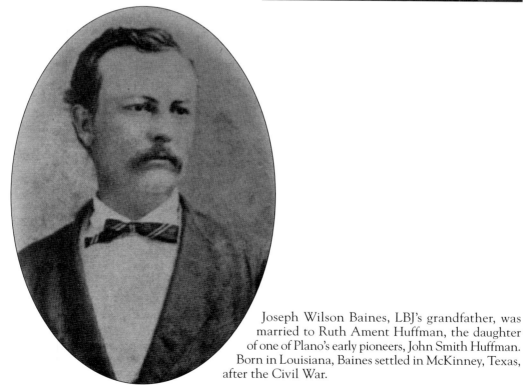

Joseph Wilson Baines, LBJ's grandfather, was married to Ruth Ament Huffman, the daughter of one of Plano's early pioneers, John Smith Huffman. Born in Louisiana, Baines settled in McKinney, Texas, after the Civil War.

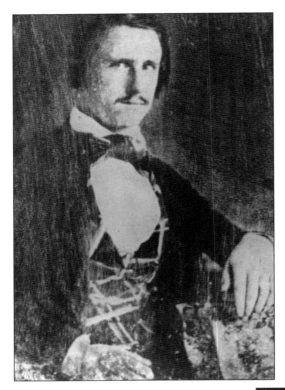

John Smith Huffman Jr., LBJ's great-grandfather, was the city of Plano's first physician. Huffman served as a surgeon for the Confederacy and returned to Texas in poor health, his nerves shattered by the horrors of war. He died in 1856 at the age of 40.

Rebekah Baines Johnson was LBJ's mother. Rebekah, the daughter of Joseph Wilson Baines and Ruth Ament Huffman, was born in the Rowlett Creek area of Plano. After Texas governor John Ireland appointed her father secretary of state in 1883, the family moved to Austin. When Joseph's term was up, the family moved to Blanco in 1887.

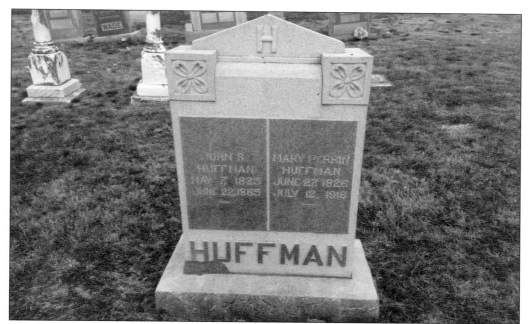

Pictured above is the John Smith Huffman Jr. and Mary Elizabeth Huffman monument at Rowlett Creek Cemetery. Mary Elizabeth would outlive John by over 50 years. The final resting place for Lyndon B. Johnson's great-great-grandfather is at Rowlett Creek Cemetery. John Smith Huffman Sr. was born in Bourbon County, Texas, on November 2, 1794. He died in the Plano area on October 7, 1880.

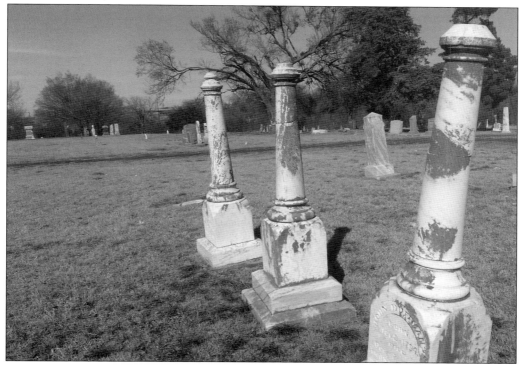

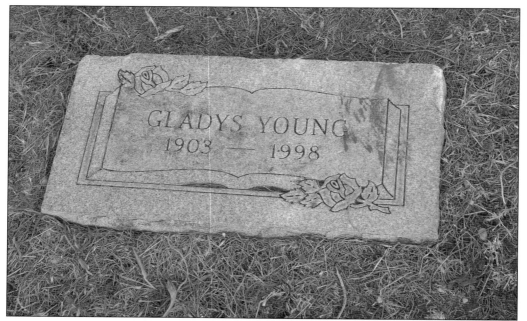

Gladys Young was the last surviving member of the Young family. The Youngs were one of the original Plano pioneer families. They settled over 300 acres in the Rowlett Creek area. Gladys was known for planting yellow irises, lilies, and jonquils around the old family farmhouse. Some of these flowers were transferred to nearby Young Cemetery, where they bloom every spring.

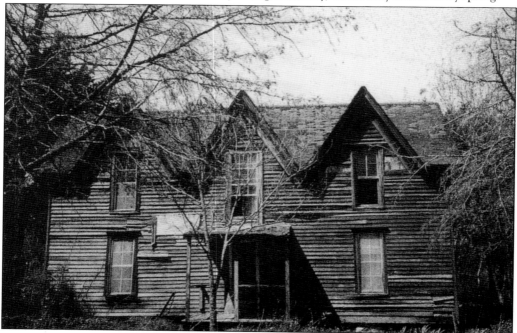

Gladys Young lived a mile west of Rowlett Cemetery in the Young house. Gladys lived in this home all her life, and in all that time the home never had indoor plumbing. It was built by Gladys and her father, Samuel, who moved to the Plano area in the 1840s.

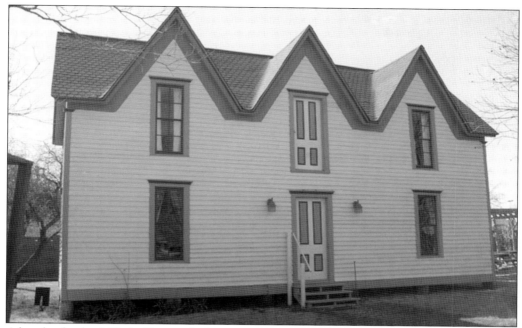

After the death of Gladys Young, the home was moved to the Heritage Farmstead Museum. The house went through an extensive restoration. It can be seen and toured at the farmstead, which is located at 1900 West Fifteenth Street in Plano, Texas.

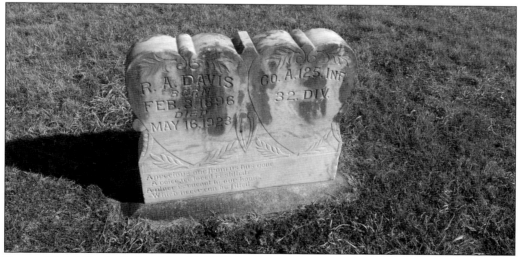

Rupert "R.A." Davis died on May 16, 1923, but he was fortunate not to lose his life years before. Davis was one of the over 2,000 American troops aboard the *Tuscania* in 1918. The *Tuscania* was a luxury liner that became a troop transporter when World War I started. The ship left Hoboken, New Jersey, on January 24, 1918. Because of a severe illness, Davis was taken off the ship in Halifax, Nova Scotia, before it made its final voyage across the Atlantic. A few days later, on February 5, 1918, the *Tuscania* was sunk by a German U-boat just off the coast of Ireland. The ship's lifeboats and escorting destroyers were able to save the majority of the troops and crew, but over 200 men lost their lives that day. Davis's illness saved him from a harrowing ordeal that may have cost him his life.

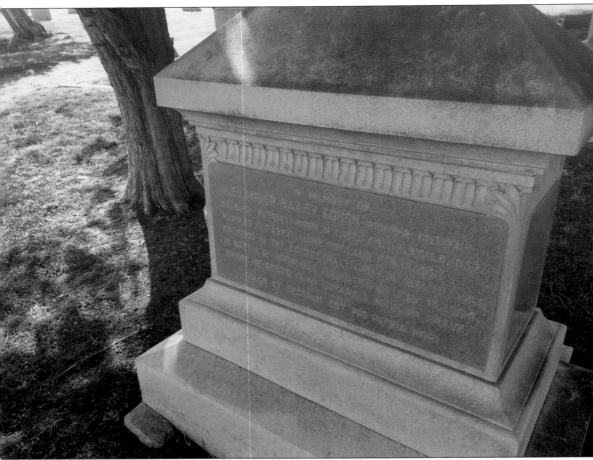

Rowlett Creek Cemetery contains a memorial to someone who is not actually buried in the cemetery. Alexander Bailey Gough moved south from his birthplace in Green County, Illinois. In 1861, at the outbreak of the Civil War, he joined the Confederacy. In 1864, he died in the Battle of Yellow Bayou (also known as Norwood's Plantation) in Louisiana. His body lies there in an unmarked grave, while his memorial is in Plano.

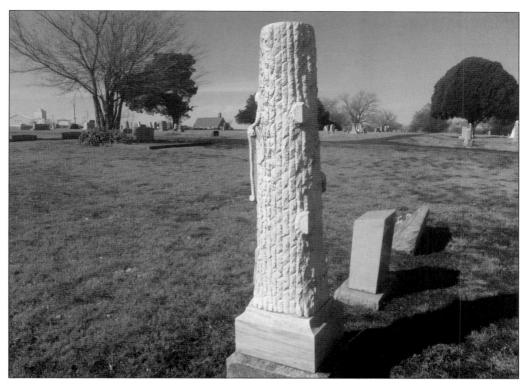

Monuments such as these from the Woodmen of the World are seen all across the United States. Founded in 1890, the Woodmen of the World is still based in its founding city of Omaha, Nebraska. The Woodmen of the World is a fraternal organization that offers benefits such as life insurance to its members. One of the benefits of Woodmen of the World membership was the easily recognized tree stump cemetery monument. This program was abandoned by Woodmen of the World in the late 1920s, as it proved to be too costly for the organization to continue. Still, the tree stump monuments are a lasting physical legacy of the Woodmen of the World.

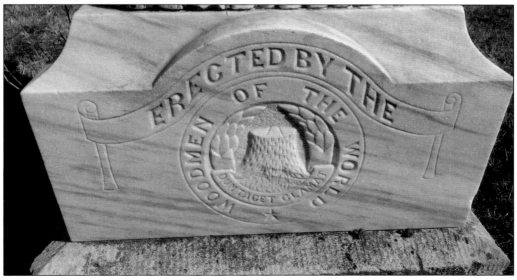

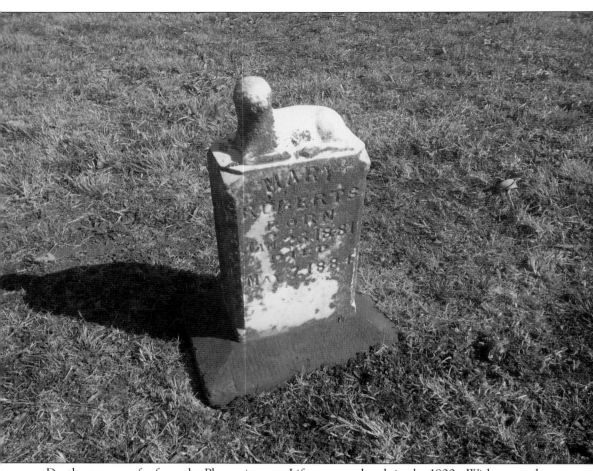

Death was never far from the Plano pioneers. Life was very harsh in the 1800s. Without modern medicine, today's minor ailments could be deadly for pioneers on the Black Land Prairie. Children were very susceptible to illness and death. The lamb motif is commonly found on the gravestones of children because of its connotation of innocence.

Seven

Young Cemetery and Scatter Garden

The Young Cemetery was begun in 1847 with the death of Patience Ann Cornell Young. The one-acre site was set aside for family members and friends who helped settle the area near the present-day crossroads of Plano, Frisco, and Allen. The cemetery, located one mile west of Rowlett Creek Cemetery, the final resting place of Gladys Young and her mother, second wife of John Young, son of Samuel Young. Three veterans lie at rest in Young Cemetery, including Thomas Finley, who fought in the War of 1812, along with Jacob Baccus and Jacob Houts, who fought for the South in the Civil War. Most of the folks buried in Young Cemetery are related by blood or marriage. The headright of Jacob Baccus included the land around the cemetery, which remained in the family until the 1970s. The cemetery is now under the care of the Young Family Cemetery Association and is recognized as a Historic Texas Cemetery by the Texas Historical Commission.

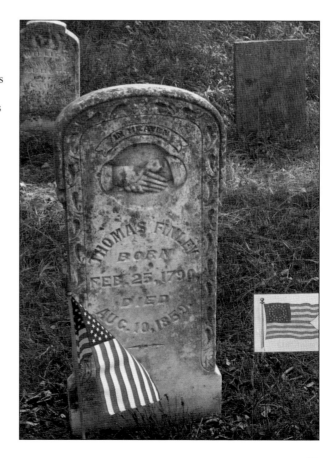

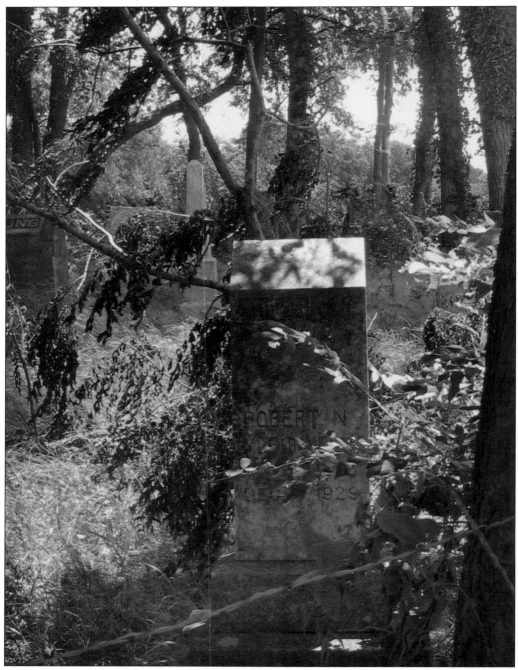

Young Cemetery suffered neglect when development and storms blocked entry for volunteers who took over its care after Gladys Young's death in 1998.

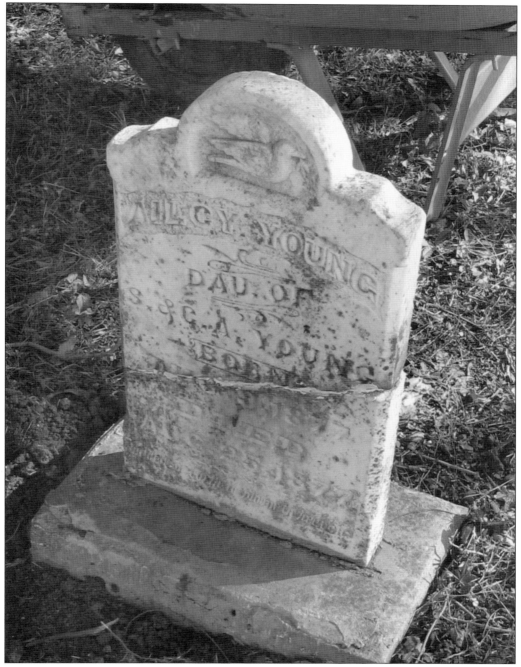

Ailcy Young's broken headstone was probably damaged by a fallen tree limb. An old, large pecan tree shades the south side of the cemetery and frequently drops debris.

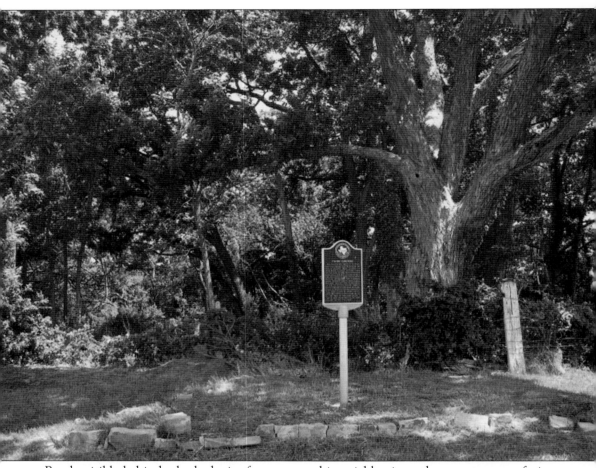

Barely visible behind a barbed wire fence covered in prickly vines, the cemetery was facing extinction threatened by development and neglect.

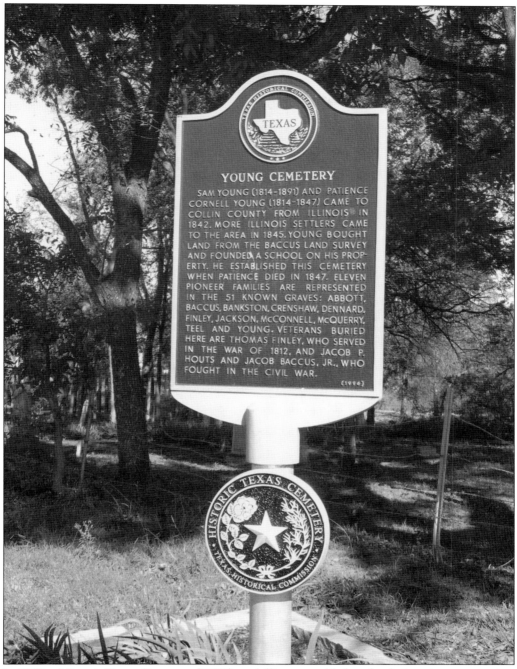

YOUNG CEMETERY

SAM YOUNG (1814-1891) AND PATIENCE
CORNELL YOUNG (1814-1847) CAME TO
COLLIN COUNTY FROM ILLINOIS IN
1842. MORE ILLINOIS SETTLERS CAME
TO THE AREA IN 1845. YOUNG BOUGHT
LAND FROM THE BACCUS LAND SURVEY
AND FOUNDED A SCHOOL ON HIS PROP-
ERTY. HE ESTABLISHED THIS CEMETERY
WHEN PATIENCE DIED IN 1847. ELEVEN
PIONEER FAMILIES ARE REPRESENTED
IN THE 51 KNOWN GRAVES: ABBOTT,
BACCUS, BANKSTON, CRENSHAW, DENNARD,
FINLEY, JACKSON, McCONNELL, McQUERRY,
TEEL AND YOUNG. VETERANS BURIED
HERE ARE THOMAS FINLEY, WHO SERVED
IN THE WAR OF 1812, AND JACOB P.
HOUTS AND JACOB BACCUS, JR., WHO
FOUGHT IN THE CIVIL WAR.

(1998)

In 2009, a Historic Texas Cemetery (HTC) medallion was added to the designations, protecting
the site and attached to the historical marker erected in 1998.

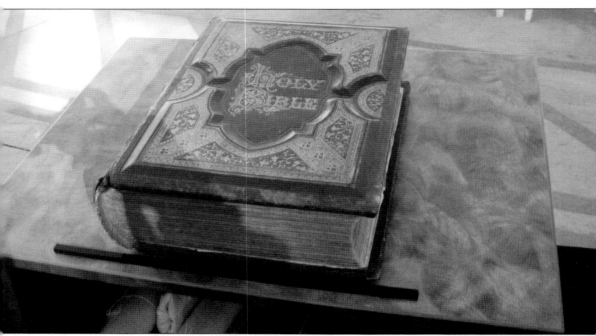

The Young family Bible was brought to the dedication ceremony of the HTC medallion in October 2009.

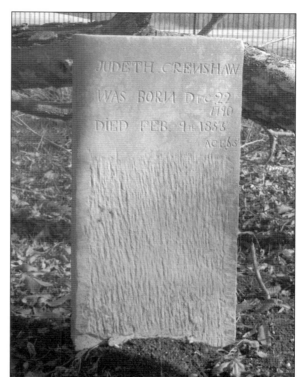

Judith Crenshaw's headstone reflects the handmade quality and lack of formal education of the inscriber. Note the reversed letter "N." Contrary to many of her contemporaries, she lived a relatively long life. Thomas Finley's original stone is pictured as it appears in modern times, hand scribed and separated from its base.

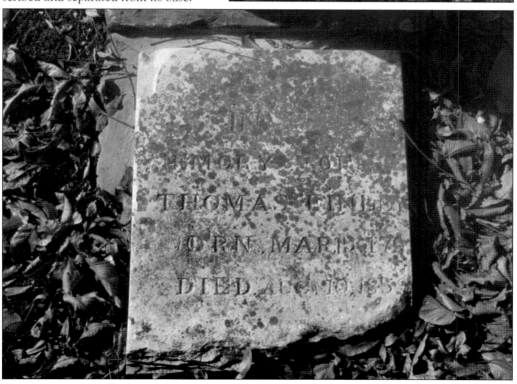

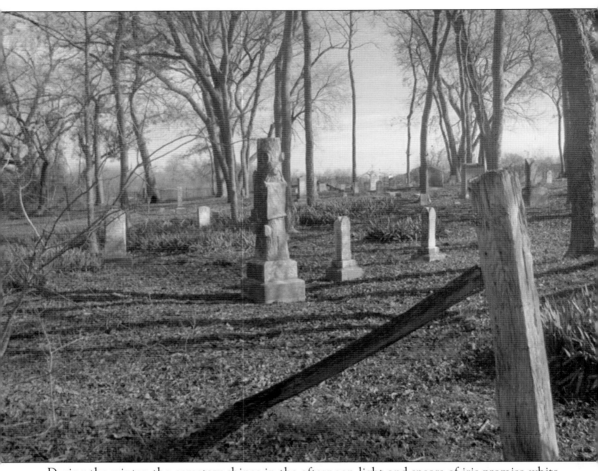

During the winter, the cemetery shines in the afternoon light and spears of iris promise white blooms in spring. The original gate posts still stand at the western edge of the burials, as seen in the foreground of this image.

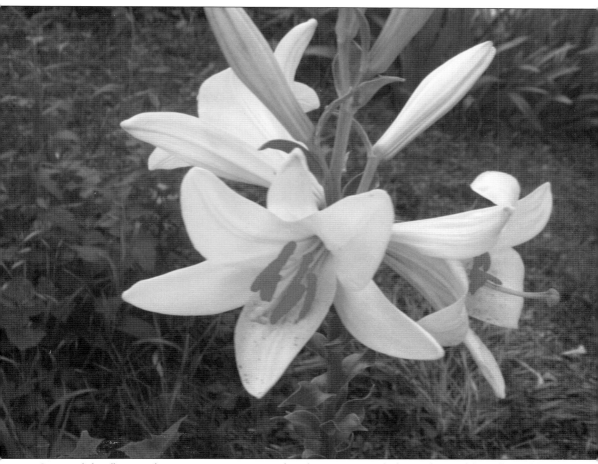

Some of the flowers that appear in spring and early summer include Madonna lilies planted by Gladys Young long ago.

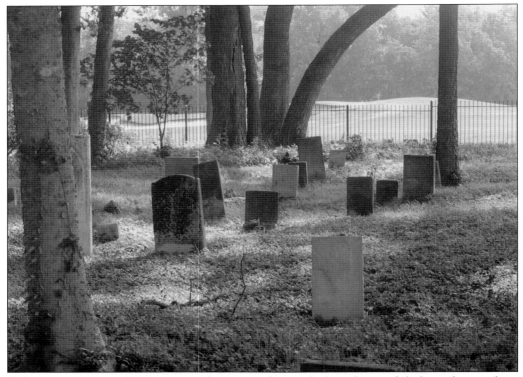

Before renovations in 2011, grave markers were askew and tilting from soil shifting, damage from weathering, and downed trees. After repairs and leveling, markers again are upright and legible.

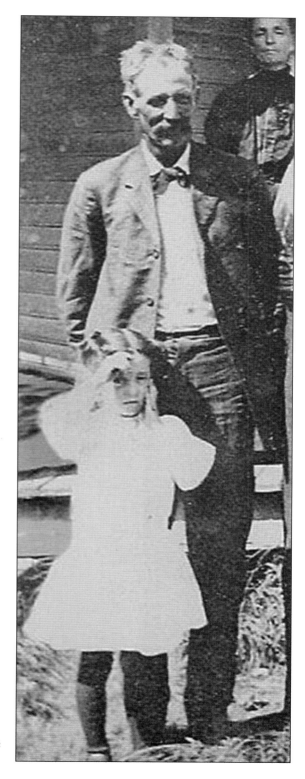

John and Gladys Young are pictured here around 1907. (Courtesy L.J. Gough.)

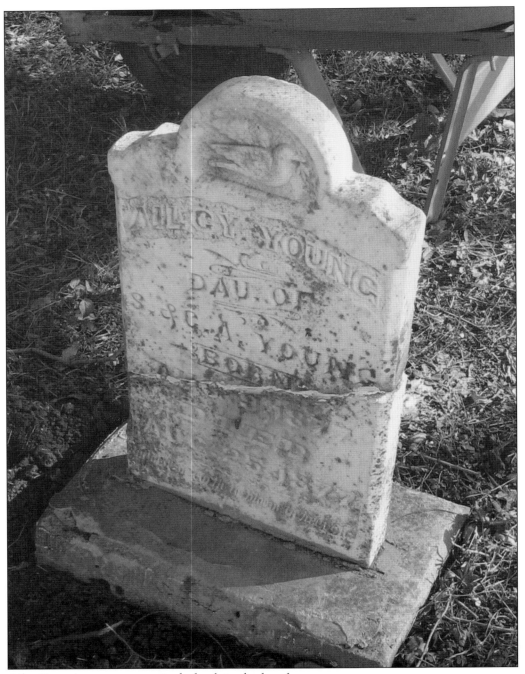

Ailcy Young's stone was repaired after lying broken for many years.

Adam Teel's marker, an iconic Woodmen of the World monument, is the tallest in the cemetery. The inscription includes the Latin "Dum Tacet Clamat" (translated "Though Silent He Speaks"), and the monument is carved as a highly ornamented tree trunk.

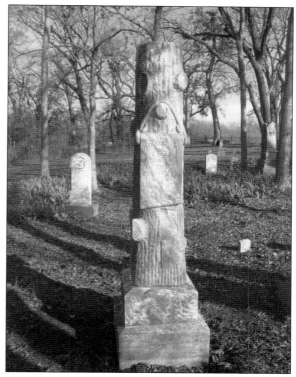

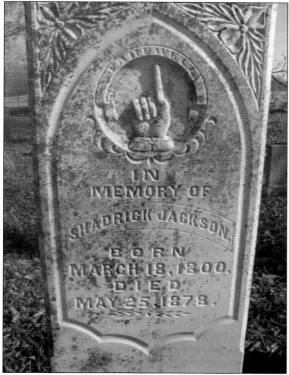

Shadrick Jackson was a charter member of the Rowlett Creek Baptist Church, whose graveyard is a mile to the east, near the terminus of the Young Branch. His son gave part of their headright to form the cemetery in 1861. The Jackson family lived near the Finleys in Madison County, Illinois, before coming to Texas. Shadrick's wife was Prudence Finley, and her headstone is nearby but much different in style and stone.

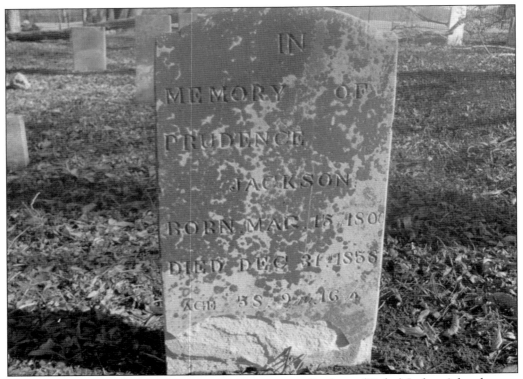

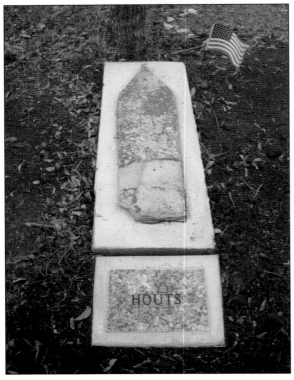

Prudence (Finley) Jackson's headstone is hand carved and much less ornate than her husband's marker. Prudence's father was John "Fighting Jack" Finley, who fought in the War of 1812, as did her brother Thomas. Jacob P. Houts's handmade marker is now unable to stand on its own and the inscription is wearing away fast. A replacement granite marker with his surname was added so his location in the cemetery would not be forgotten. Houts was part of Company G of the Texas Regiment during the Civil War.

The cemetery now offers a scatter garden. Funds collected from the scatter garden fees help continue the preservation and protection of the historic cemetery grounds. A new granite monument remembers those "who have gone before."

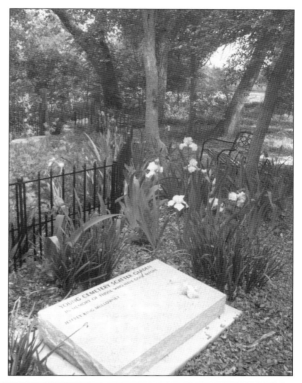

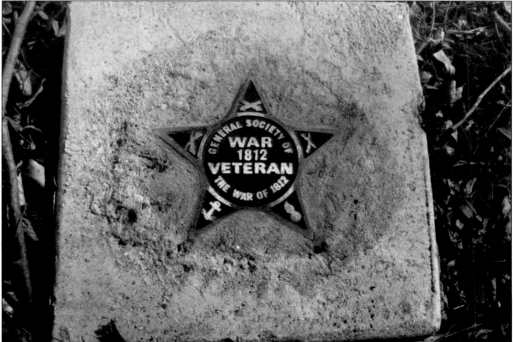

In 2010, the CAR Chapter of the General Society of the War of 1812 installed and dedicated a bronze star to honor Thomas Finley's service during that war.

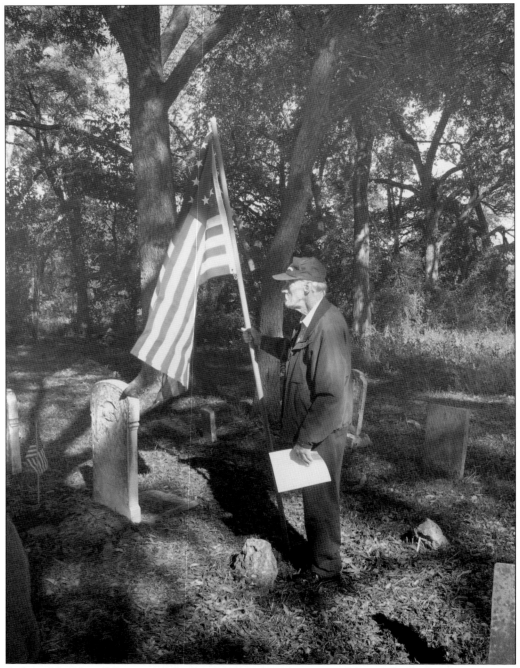

A flag of the United States used during the War of 1812 was carried during the dedication ceremony for Thomas Finley's marker by a member of the General Society in November 2010.

Eight

COLLINSWORTH CEMETERY

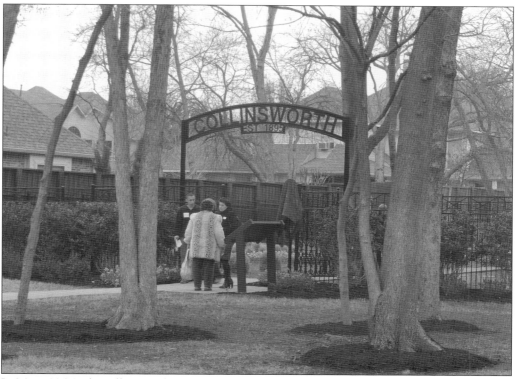

In May 1895, Milt Collinsworth welcomed a traveling salesman into his home for the night—an act of hospitality that would dramatically impact the family's future. The next morning, as the man was leaving, he mentioned not feeling well. A young Collinsworth daughter who helped to change the sheets of the bed in which the man slept became sick and was diagnosed with smallpox.

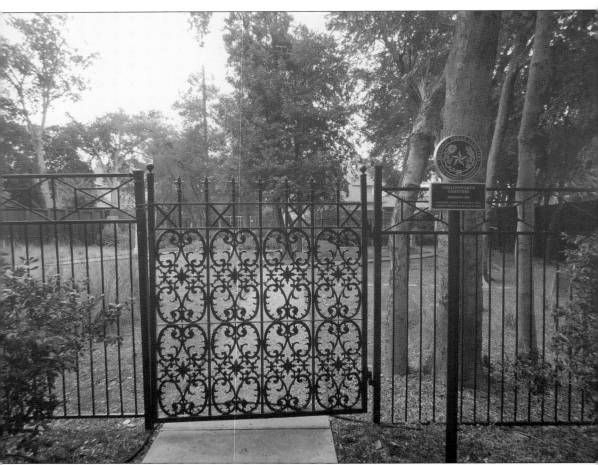

During this time, it was traditional to have an at-home funeral. It was also still common practice to have each person pass by the body individually to pay his or her final respects. These traditions greatly enhanced the spread of smallpox, and the Collinsworth family was tragically one of the prairie families that lost many of its members.

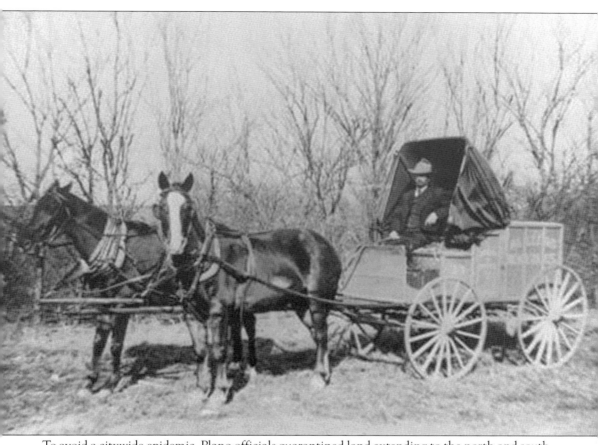

To avoid a citywide epidemic, Plano officials quarantined land extending to the north and south, by present-day Spring Creek Parkway and Park Boulevard and to the east and west by what is now Coit Road and Preston Road. Passage on all through roads was prohibited, making transport of food and medical supplies very difficult.

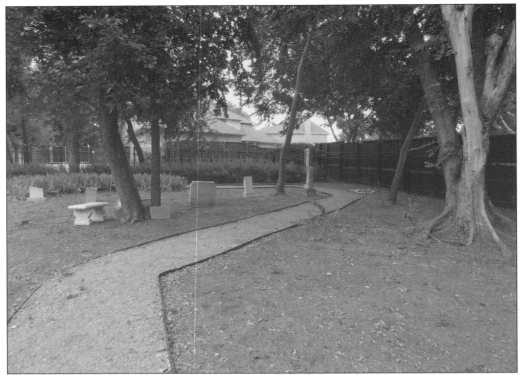

Only a few compassionate friends and those who had already recovered from smallpox crossed the quarantine to come to the aid of the Collinsworth family. There is a surviving oral history that claims, even years after the epidemic had passed, the Collinsworth girls did not enjoy going into town because the other people there would treat them with fear and suspicion.

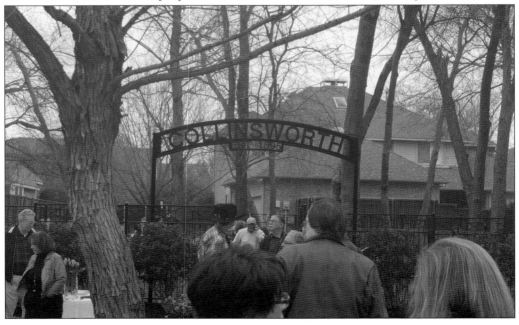

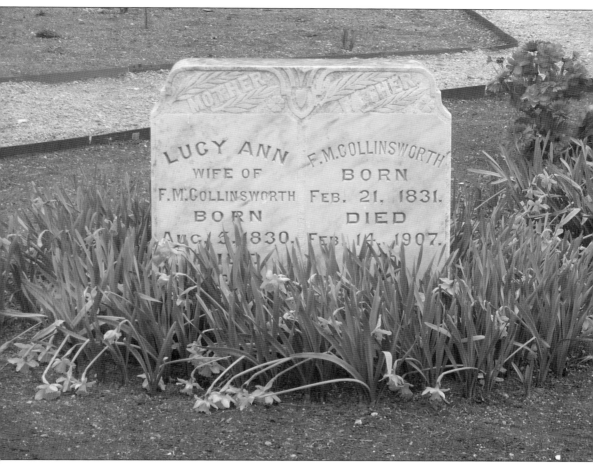

MOTHER TOGETHER

LUCY ANN   F.M.COLLINSWORTH
WIFE OF   BORN
F.M.COLLINSWORTH FEB. 21, 1831.
BORN   DIED
AUG. 3, 1830. FEB. 14, 1907.

Even when a smallpox diagnosis came early, many doctors, including the one that treated the Collinsworths, were unfamiliar with proper measures of treatment. Once the disease began to spread through the family, there were four deaths within the first two weeks. Eventually, over 15 relatives succumbed to the illness.

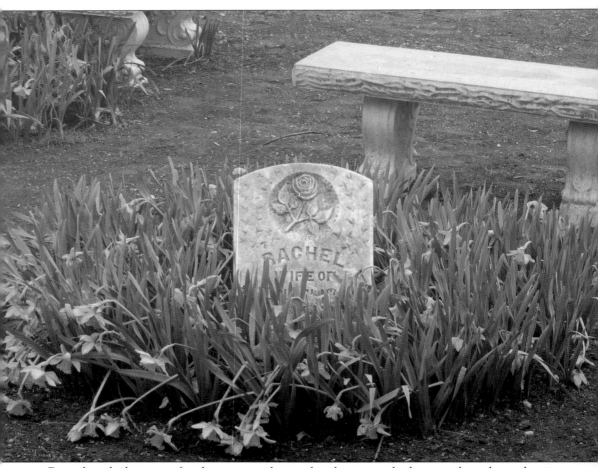

Even though this was a family cemetery during this short time, bodies were brought to the site from as far away as Frisco and buried at night, a practice thought to help lessen the likelihood of contamination.

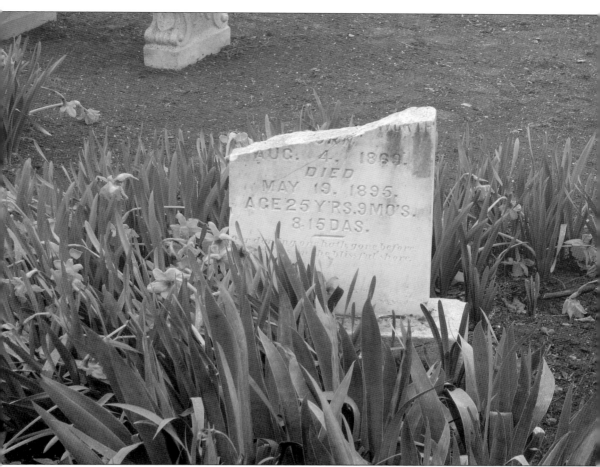

BORN
AUG. 4, 1869.
DIED
MAY 19, 1895.
AGE 25 YRS. 9 MO'S.
8-15 DAS.

Although five stones are visible in the Collinsworth Cemetery, reports cite this as the resting place for as many as 30 Collinsworth family members, and it is recorded that the site was used as late as 1925 for a family member's burial. Local road development left the location of the cemetery downhill of major roads.

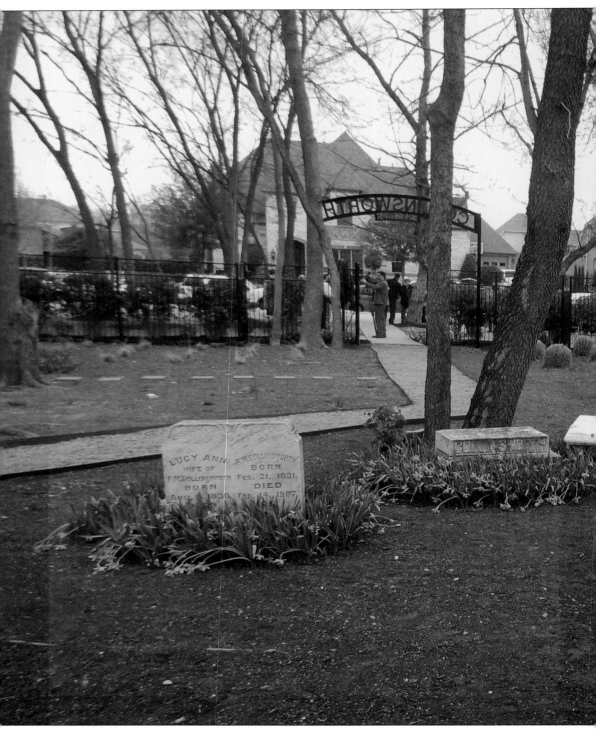

Rainfall and exposure left the cemetery covered in heavy mud, and dedicated volunteers worked to recover what stones they could. Many stones have disappeared, leaving the possibility that

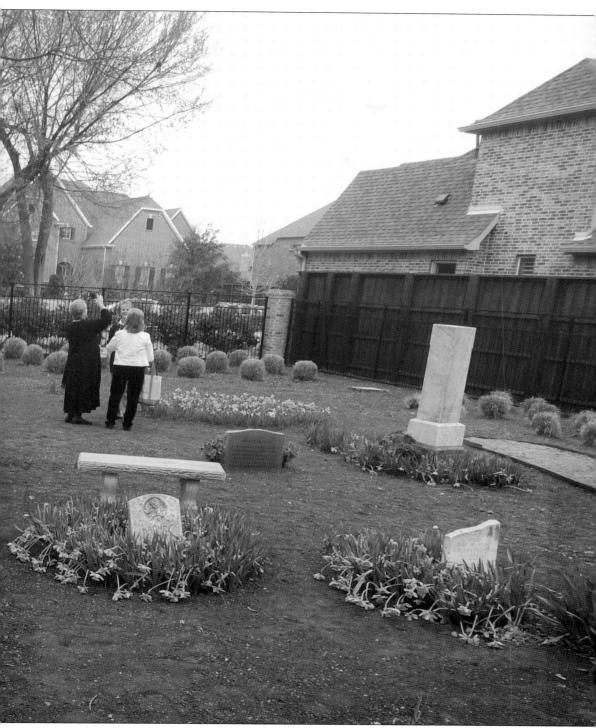

some are buried under as much as 18 inches of soil that still covers the original cemetery.

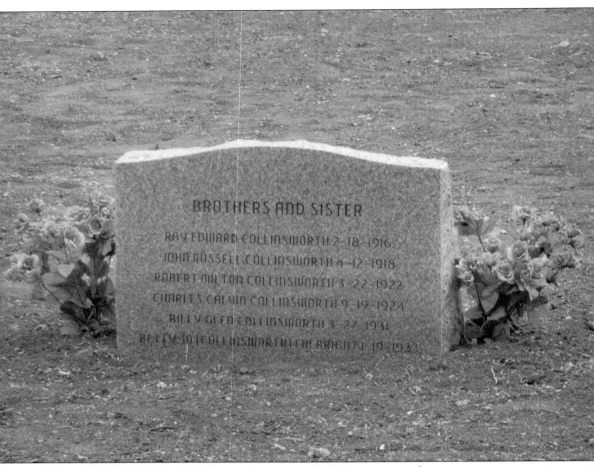

BROTHERS AND SISTER

RAY EDWARD COLLINSWORTH 2-18-1916
JOHN RUSSELL COLLINSWORTH 4-12-1918
ROBERT MILTON COLLINSWORTH 3-22-1922
CHARLES CALVIN COLLINSWORTH 9-19-1924
BILLY GLEN COLLINSWORTH 3-27-1931
BETTY JO [COLLINSWORTH] [FULBRIGHT] 1-19-1933

Due to the loss of the original monuments, people have come together to create a new stone that honors multiple people who are buried at the cemetery. This is becoming a more common process for descendants and community members as cemeteries are aging and preservation efforts are beginning to take off.

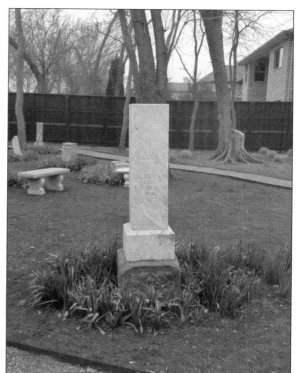

On March 8, 2014, people gathered for the official unveiling of the Texas Historic Site medallion at the front gate of the cemetery. The event was also a celebration to honor those who have worked so hard at restoring and maintaining the cemetery throughout the years.

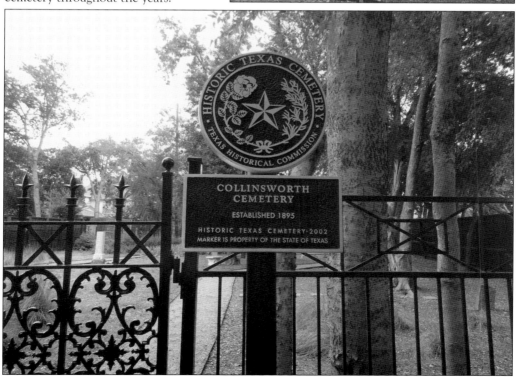

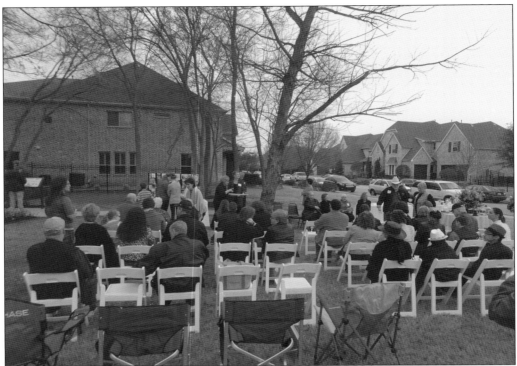

Many descendants of the Collinsworth family drove in from all over the state to attend the event, hosted by Charlotte A. Carpenter Johnson and Kathy Nelson. It served as a wonderful symbol of what can be accomplished when people work together at preserving important pieces of Plano's heritage.

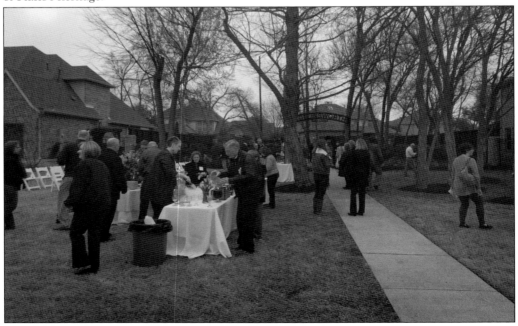

Nine

ADDITIONAL HISTORIC PLANO CEMETERIES

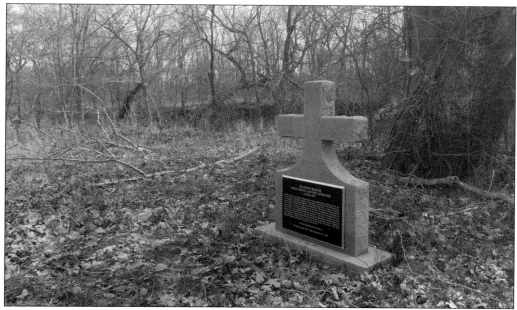

This monument commemorates the unmarked graves of the victims of the Muncey Incident. Two Plano pioneers—McBain Jamison and Jeremiah Muncey—settled near this site in the 1840s. In the fall of 1844, two other Plano pioneers—Leonard Searcy and William Rice—were out hunting when they decided to pay a visit to the Muncey family. What they found were the brutally destroyed bodies of McBain Jamison, Jeremiah Muncey, Mrs. Muncey, and their small child. Searcy and Rice quickly left the killing site to find their own sons, who were out hunting in the area. In a cruel twist of fate, Rice's son was found dead but Searcy's son was safe. Two of Muncey's sons were never found.

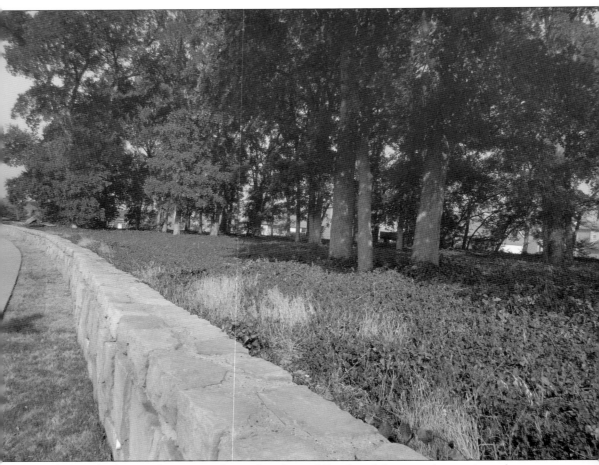

The Leach-Thomas Cemetery is located in the middle of a subdivision. At one time, there were over 100 graves in this cemetery, but now, only four stones remain. One of the oldest and still-standing stones is that of Preston Lawrence Leach, who was born in 1824 and died January 8, 1868. He was a pioneer settler and became a Texas partisan ranger for the Confederate army.

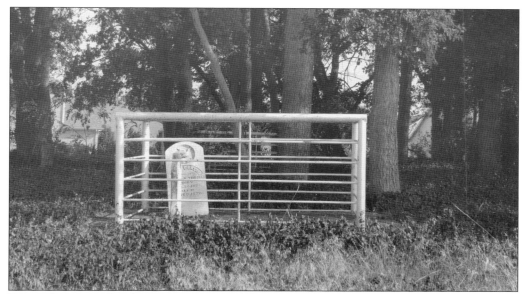

Preston Lawrence Leach came to Texas with his wife and eight children. Preston and his eldest son both enlisted in the Confederate army. When Preston's wife, Elizabeth, died in 1895, she unfortunately passed away during a terrible rainstorm, and although her family had intentions of burying her at Leach-Thomas, they were forced to stop at the Allen Cemetery. The family had to bury Elizabeth in Allen because the roads were full of mud and had become treacherous. Her grave is near the entrance of the Allen Cemetery.

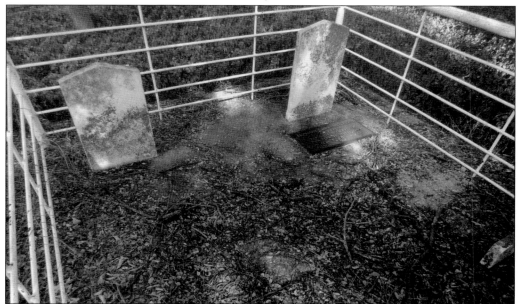

Although Leach-Thomas is a small cemetery, its legacy ties it to one of America's largest political figures, Lyndon B. Johnson. When William Perrin divided his land among his children, his daughter (Mrs. Thomas) inherited property on which the cemetery was located. Another Perrin daughter, Mary Elizabeth, married John Smith Huffman Jr., who was the first doctor in Plano. They are now buried in Rowlett Cemetery and were the great-grandparents of LBJ.

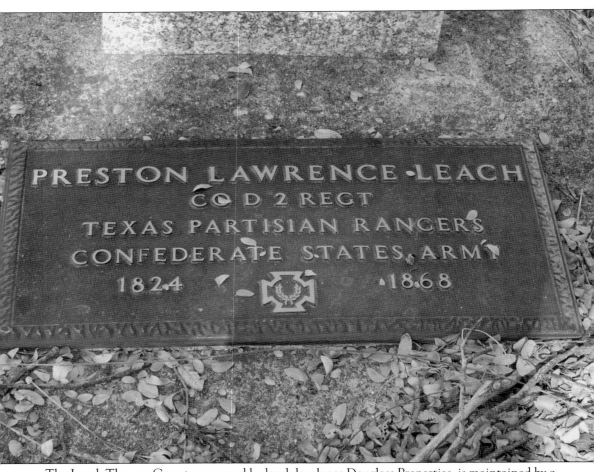

PRESTON LAWRENCE LEACH
CO D 2 REGT
TEXAS PARTISIAN RANGERS
CONFEDERATE STATES ARMY
1824   1868

The Leach-Thomas Cemetery, owned by land developer Douglass Properties, is maintained by a clause in the now surrounding subdivision's homeowners association charter. Douglass believes in accommodating the cemetery rather than hiding it, claiming "you can't ignore it or hide it in somebody's backyard. You have to acknowledge that it's there," as quoted on the cemetery's website. The Plano Conservancy for Historic Preservation, Inc. has stated that its mission within the coming years is to be involved in the efforts to get the remaining monuments restored and protected, as well as cleaning the grounds and painting the cattle guard fence.

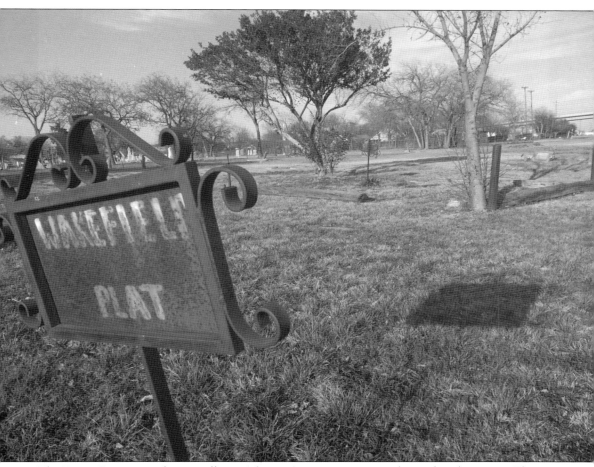

The Davis Cemetery is historically an African American cemetery located in downtown Plano. The cemetery lies adjacent to the Old City Cemetery on its southern boundary.

MY REMEMBERS

A
Black
Sharecropper's
Recollections
of the
Depression

Eddie Stimpson, Jr. ("Sarge")
Introduction by James Byrd

Eddie Stimpson Jr. was an African American sharecropper in Plano, Texas. His book *My Remembers: A Black Sharecropper's Recollections of the Depression* tells the story of his experiences on farms in Plano during the 1930s and 1940s. (Courtesy of the University of North Texas Press.)

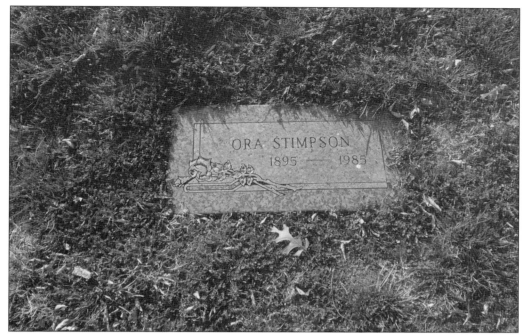

There are many members of the Stimpson family buried in Davis Cemetery. Ora Stimpson, who was born in 1895 and died in 1985, would have shared the same Depression era–experiences as Eddie Stimpson Jr.

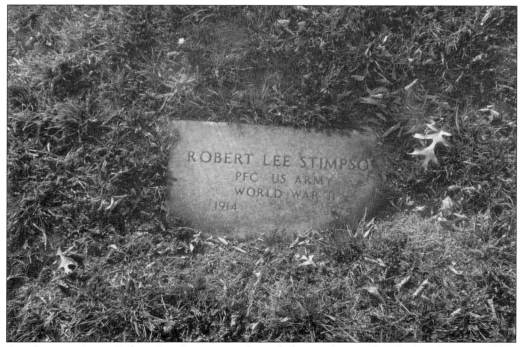

Ora Stimpson's son Robert Lee Stimpson is buried close to his mother. Robert Lee served his country in World War II in the US Army.

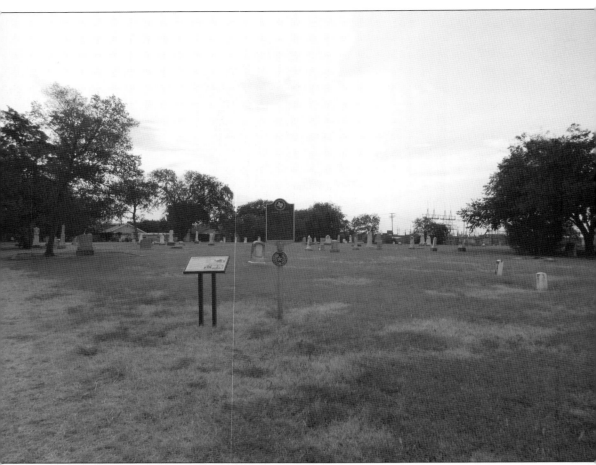

Old City Cemetery is sometimes known as the Pioneer Cemetery; this large burial ground was designated for such use in 1848. The cemetery was associated with the earliest Methodist church in Plano, where worshippers gathered until 1894. Five Peters Colonists, the original Plano pioneers, are buried in this cemetery.

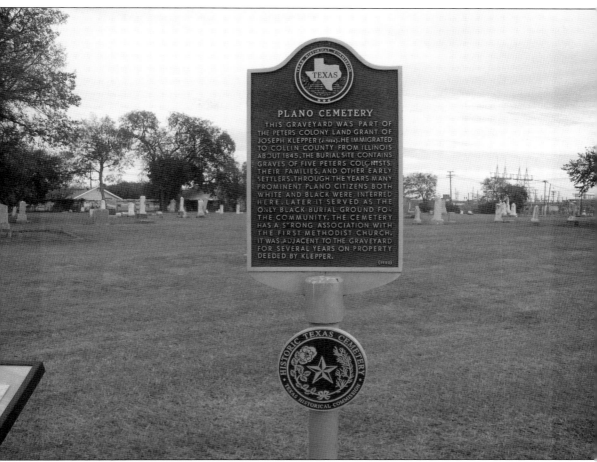

Old City Cemetery has a unique African American history. Over the years, the original Peters Colony neighborhood, for which the cemetery was built, evolved into an African American community, resulting in Old City Cemetery becoming one of the first integrated cemeteries in the state of Texas.

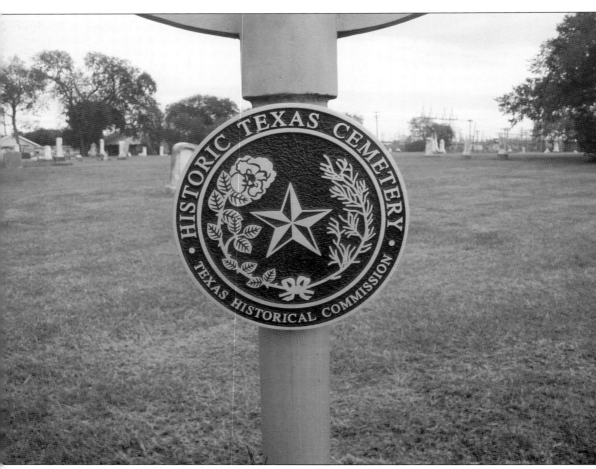

Old City Cemetery is a designated Historic Texas Cemetery. According to the Texas Historical Commission, "the Historic Texas Cemetery designation was developed in 1998 to help protect historic cemeteries by recording cemetery boundaries in county deed records to alert present and future owners of land adjacent to the cemetery of its existence. Every county in Texas has at least one cemetery designated as a Historic Texas Cemetery through this program. The HTC designation is the first step toward preservation of a historic cemetery."

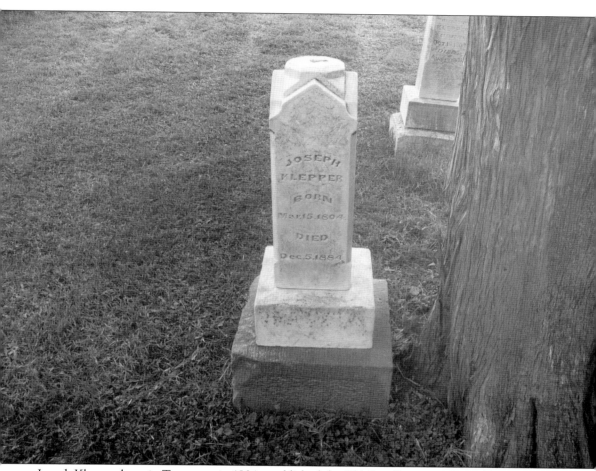

Joseph Klepper, born in Tennessee in 1804, established the Old City Cemetery. One of the original Peters Colonists, he came to the Plano area in the 1840s. Klepper married Nancy Beverly in Granger County, Tennessee, in 1829.

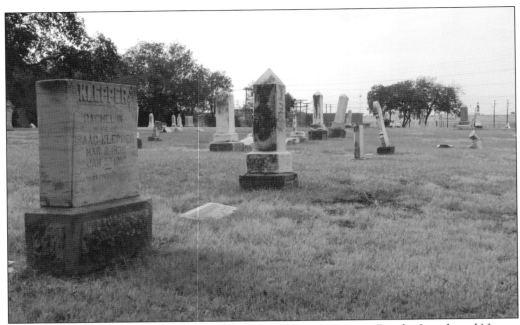

Six members of the Klepper family are buried in Old City Cemetery. Besides Joseph and Nancy, there are Andrew, Daniel Boone, and Isaac (son of Joseph) and his wife, Rachel.

FUNERAL NOTICE

The friends and acquaintances of John S. Good and family are requested to attend the funeral of his wife

MRS. JULIA A. GOOD

(born October 16th, 1853, departed this life September 14th, 1907, at 5 o'clock a. m.)

Funeral services at First Baptist church tomorrow (Sunday) evening at 3 o'clock, conducted by Rev. H. N. G. Bentley.

     Interment in the City cemetery.

Plano, Texas, Sept. 14th, 1907.

This is a funeral notice for Julia Good, buried at Old City Cemetery in 1907. The notice requests that the family and acquaintances of John Good attend the funeral for his wife.

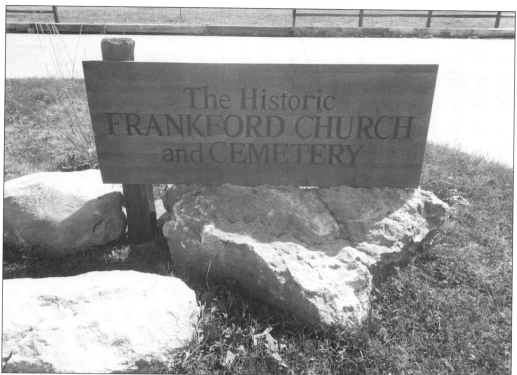

Frankford Cemetery is situated in far southwestern Collin County and named for the tiny farming community of Frankford, settled in the 1850s. The town grew near Indian Springs, a source of water for travelers in the area for hundreds of years. The first known unmarked grave in the cemetery dates to 1862. It is possible there are earlier burials in Frankford Cemetery, and there is some speculation that Native Americans are buried there as well. Some of Plano's early settlers are buried in Frankford Cemetery.

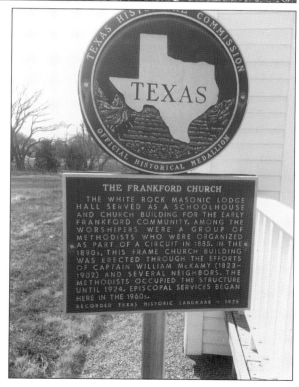

THE FRANKFORD CHURCH

THE WHITE ROCK MASONIC LODGE HALL SERVED AS A SCHOOLHOUSE AND CHURCH BUILDING FOR THE EARLY FRANKFORD COMMUNITY. AMONG THE WORSHIPERS WERE A GROUP OF METHODISTS WHO WERE ORGANIZED AS PART OF A CIRCUIT IN 1885. IN THE 1890s, THIS FRAME CHURCH BUILDING WAS ERECTED THROUGH THE EFFORTS OF CAPTAIN WILLIAM McKAMY (1823–1902) AND SEVERAL NEIGHBORS. THE METHODISTS OCCUPIED THE STRUCTURE UNTIL 1924. EPISCOPAL SERVICES BEGAN HERE IN THE 1960s.
RECORDED TEXAS HISTORIC LANDMARK – 1978

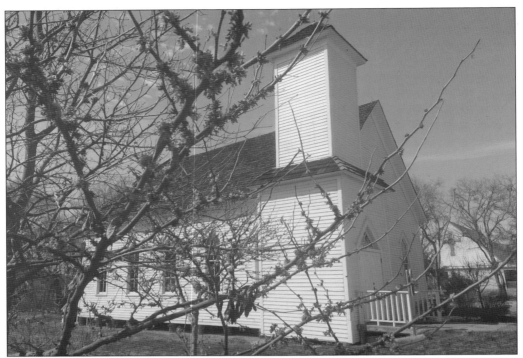

In 2010, the Frankford Cemetery Association completed a faithful restoration of the church. Citing the "elegance of its simplicity," Preservation Dallas awarded Frankford Church its Preservation Achievement Award. The Frankford Cemetery Association continues to preserve and protect the church, cemetery, wagon yard, and historic prairie.

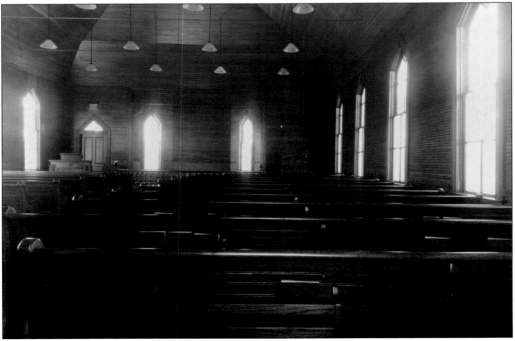

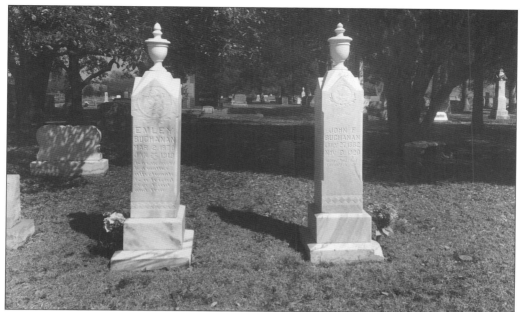

There are many famous names that found their final resting places in the beautiful Frankford Cemetery. Henry William Coit, whom Coit Road would be named after, was laid to rest here. According to Frankford Cemetery's website, "Every third Sunday in May lot owners decorated graves in the cemetery and had a Dinner on the Grounds followed by a simple service in the little church. In 1948 Frankford Cemetery Association was incorporated under the condition that a certain number of Lodge members serve on the Board of Directors. In the 1990s the FCA and White Rock Masonic Lodge parted ways giving the FCA total ownership of the cemetery, church, and grounds."

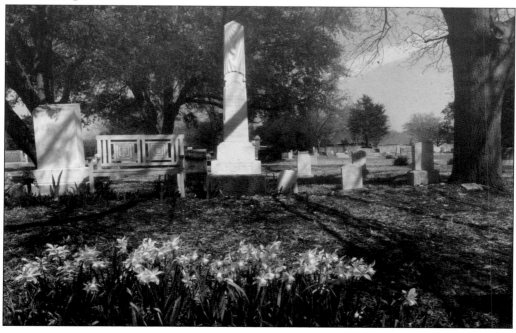

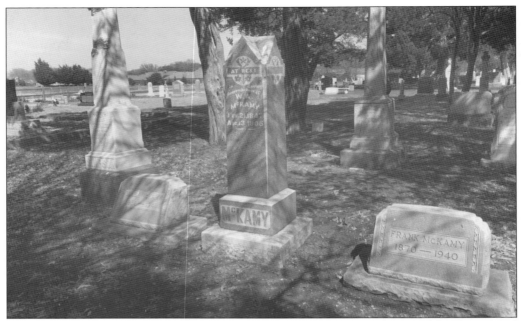

In 1852, Capt. William Clinton McKamy and Rachel McKamy arrived at Frankford by covered wagon. In the late 1890s, Captain McKamy paid to build the current Frankford Church on land he had previously sold to the White Rock Masonic Lodge to replace a former church that was destroyed by a tornado mid-construction in the 1870s.

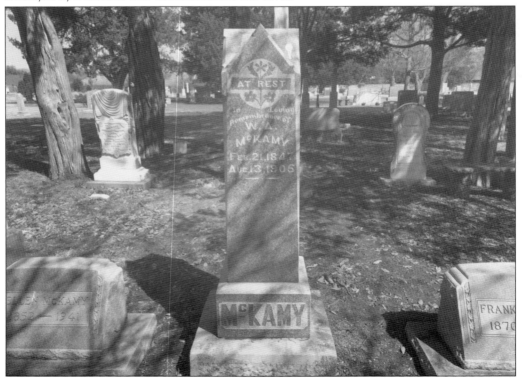

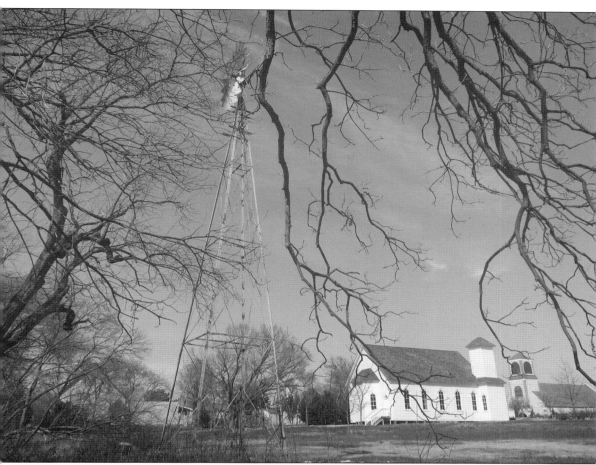

The native big bluestem grass (pioneers called it "turkey foot") will not grow in soil that has been worked for agriculture. The one-room Frankford Church is surrounded by rippling fields of prairie grass that a consulting naturalist believes have never been plowed. This untouched land serves as a physical touchstone to the area's past, much in the way the cemeteries themselves remain in tribute to those brave settlers who lived, loved, worked, and passed away on the prairie.

DISCOVER THOUSANDS OF LOCAL HISTORY BOOKS FEATURING MILLIONS OF VINTAGE IMAGES

Arcadia Publishing, the leading local history publisher in the United States, is committed to making history accessible and meaningful through publishing books that celebrate and preserve the heritage of America's people and places.

Find more books like this at
www.arcadiapublishing.com

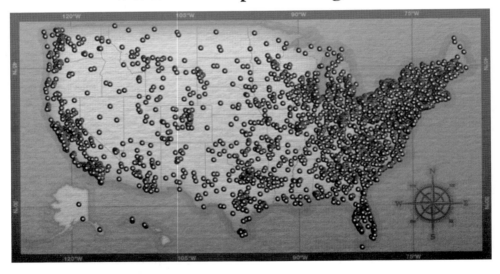

Search for your hometown history, your old stomping grounds, and even your favorite sports team.

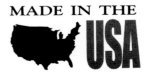